Sh

Shining in Plain View

John Wheeler

NON-DUALITY PRESS

NON-DUALITY PRESS

6 Folkestone Road Salisbury SP2 8JP United Kingdom

www.non-dualitybooks.com

ISBN 0-9547792-6-6

Preface

I am happy that Julian Noyce of Non-Duality Press has agreed to bring out a second book of dialogues and articles as a follow up to my first book *Awakening to the Natural State*. I am pleased to see that growing numbers of people are resonating with the simple yet profound message which has come down to us through Sri Nisargadatta Maharaj and his student 'Sailor' Bob Adamson. The good news is that there can be an end to doubts, suffering and seeking through a clear understanding of our true nature, that simple and undeniable presence of existence, awareness and love that is always present and shining at our centre. This is the ancient message of Advaita or non-duality presented in a contemporary form, a form that can be easily understood and experienced by people leading normal lives in the modern world.

The key point of this approach is that the truth we are seeking is already present as our own actual being. A little bit of investigation reveals that what we are is really that simple sense of presence that is both existing and brightly aware. All suffering, doubts and seeking arise from not clearly recognizing who we are. Clarifying this matter, which does not take time, but only clear seeing, completely resolves all questions and doubts. What remains is a sense of clarity, certitude, peace and well-being that cannot be touched by events or circumstances.

I often speak of two facets of this understanding. The first is the clear recognition of the truth of what we are. The second is the dismantling of any false ideas about ourselves. You come to see what is true about yourself and discard what is false. These are like two sides of a single coin. They appear as two different approaches but really come back to the same core point, which is simply bringing our real identity into clear view.

The material in this book expands on these points through selections from actual dialogues and correspondence I have had with people who are deeply interested in discovering their own true nature. The reader will be delighted, as I am, to see how this understanding unfolds and becomes direct experience for those who apply themselves with earnestness, follow the pointers, and discover their own innate freedom and happiness. In the end, the words and teachings are least relevant. At best they can only point. The only one thing that matters and needs to be known, is the fact of your own being.

Since I returned from meeting 'Sailor' Bob Adamson in 2003, an increasing number of people have been able to understand the basics of what is being pointed to. Many of them are now sharing the message of freedom in their own way. It is very gratifying to see the message of freedom through self-knowledge alive and flourishing.

I want to extend my deep appreciation and thanks to Leslie Caren and Julian Noyce for their assistance in editing the book and preparing it for printing.

John Wheeler
Santa Cruz, California, 2005

Table of Contents

Things Happen Simply and Easily

Question: I wanted to write to tell you that since I last e-mailed, the personality still shows up but identifying with it has dropped away for the most part. The lack of identification has become most noticeable during what could be called problematic circumstances, when constriction or resistance arises.

There is an awareness of thoughts (about whatever the current circumstance is) appearing in the mind. However, belief in these thoughts wanes. These are usually thoughts which tell a story about how someone is wrong or hurtful or how circumstances ought to be different than they are appearing in that moment. But as a result of not investing belief in these arising thoughts, whatever action does arise feels appropriate. It is also noticeable that there is no premeditation. The responses arise naturally out of awareness. The first time I noticed this it made me laugh. It was so unexpected. The habit of premeditation, expectation and planning is really what creates the sense of time, isn't it?

Sometimes I can feel the tug to defend an identity, a 'me', but it is now more often seen as an empty and pointless habit and so it dissipates. Sometimes defense does come up, but then it is gone. In fact, aside from the thoughts that may arise out of habit, there is really only silence and present awareness in whatever is being experienced. This presence-awareness is raw and awesome. It is deeply satisfying.

Life seems to unfold effortlessly more often than not now. I can see there is no need to think about it. I can feel old habits fading somehow. Things are more peaceful. It turns out that it is really quite simple, isn't it!?

John: What you are expressing is wonderful. The understanding of your true nature unfolds spontaneously and naturally. The insights you are sharing show that the basics have registered. From here, things do happen simply and easily. As you sit with this, the basics become clearer and the effects of peace and certainty continue to be felt. Then at some point along the way you realize that it is absolutely clear and beyond doubt. You know for certain that this peace is your natural and effortless experience. It was there all along, but overlooked. This is a very natural and organic process of understanding.

Planning for the future is fine, but it is just a relative activity. The key is that you see that the direct recognition of your nature is not some future event and it is not 'out there'. Until the basics are seen, the mind runs here, there and everywhere and thinks about the past, present and future, always hoping to find something to bring fulfillment. Then you see that what you are seeking is right here and now in the simple sense of presence in which all thoughts and experiences, including ideas of the future, arise. Then the seeking drops off because there is no need to seek what you already are. From here, any amount of activity and planning take place just fine. But there is a knowing that whatever is done or not done, you are right where you need to be. You are never apart from the reality that is shining at your core.

Can the Effects Remain?

Question: It seems that all that arises from presence-awareness is no different than presence-awareness. Fear, ideas, beliefs, the world and everything else arise as presence-awareness. Presence-awareness is one substance.

John: Yes! You have hit the nail on the head. But when you see this, the fears, doubts, and questions based on the belief in separation have no more foundation and subside. If there is no cause can the effects remain? Either way, it does not matter. All questions are resolved and you are home.

As Simple as 1 - 2 - 3

Question: John, am I on the right track?

John: Short answer: Yes!

Q: At various times during the day for the last few weeks I have been carrying out an 'awareness inquiry'. This is difficult to describe. I do not regard it as a meditation practice, but when I am sitting waiting for a bus or train, or while out walking, or just sitting at home, or indeed at any time during the day, I look and relax inwards to see if I can recognize the awareness or presence that contains everything I perceive. Sometimes it is just a looking without questions. At other times, I ask 'Who am I?' or 'What is it that has remained constant and unchanging through every moment of my life?' I relax and look inward. Anything that arises in my awareness, such as outside phenomena, sensations in my body, thoughts or feelings, is recognized as not being 'That' and the looking continues.

John: Good! It is just a natural checking in to confirm what is being pointed to. Past a point, you discover that what you are seeing is ever-present. This occurs naturally. First things are pointed out. Then we verify them for ourselves. Then it all becomes our own experience. It is as simple as 1-2-3.

Q: Lately, I have been dimly sensing a kind of space or openness that is not a physical space or openness. Also, there has been a lessening of attachments to thoughts and emotions. It appears to be the beginning of a recognition that I am not my thoughts or feelings and that I have no control over them, that indeed there is no 'I' who can possibly have any measure of control whatsoever. While most people would find the notion that there is no one doing anything to be very disturbing, I am beginning to find it liberating. Life is being lived just as before, but with a greater sense of freedom and a lessening of suffering. Fear and anxiety still arise (out of habit, I suspect), but they do not have the same grip they used to have.

John: These are excellent signs and show you are on track and that the pointing is registering.

Q: Actually, even asking 'Am I on the right track?' does not sound right because it suggests that I am on my way to somewhere that I am not already, which is clearly not the case, since it is here and now as I type this. But I hope you get the heart of my question.

John: Yes!

Q: Thanks, by the way, for the wonderful clarity of your teaching. Although the recognition is not deep yet, I am beginning to see how utterly and astoundingly simple it all is. It is so simple that saying or thinking anything about it at all complicates and obscures it.

John: Just keep in mind it is not really about depth or lack of depth. There are no levels of depth in awareness or the sense of existence. It is completely full and clear right from the start. There is no need to give any weight to the subtle concept that your recognition is not deep. When you turn to the recognition of your nature as present awareness, you see that it is really there in full from the get go. It is not a matter of progression. It is simply seeing the ever-present obvious that had been overlooked.

Whose Birthday?

Question: At the personality level, I have been in a funk since the holidays. Childhood patterns of guilt, shame and low self-esteem always seem to resurface during and after the holidays (family reunions).

John: It is just some old concepts and conditioning showing up. That is all that is going on. If you see it as such, it loses its charge. Whether that appears or not isn't the issue. The issue is what do you take yourself to be? Are you the limited, defective being the thoughts would have you believe? Or are you the simple sense of presence and awareness knowing the thoughts? When you believe in the thoughts as being true it feeds them. Settling in with the recognition of (and as) being-awareness has the effect of draining the life out of the conceptual mechanism.

Q: Today is my birthday, which brings forth feelings of sentiment and regret over the past and hope and fear for the future.

John: These are just more thoughts, along with a little belief in the reality of time for spice!

Q: Yet, I am aware that all these thoughts and feelings are happening within awareness, which remains untouched.

John: Yes. Continue to notice this and explore it.

Q: I have attempted to write you a couple times over the past weeks. But every time I started to write I became self-conscious that any question I had has already been answered in your articles, so I stop. In stopping, I had this instant of recognition that awareness has no questions. It is the answer! But this insight does not appear to stick, and I slip right back into a funk of emotional and psychological suffering. Then while going about my daily routine there comes a recognition out of the blue that no one is here (me), no one is there (other people) and nothing has happened.

John: These are the valid and true insights that start to come up naturally. This is excellent.

Q: It appears that spiritual awakening is an inner fire that, once ignited, begins to take on a life of its own, burning its way through the fabric of the minds habitual thought-patterns.

John: That sounds good.

Q: Ever since I discovered your website last year, a light within, which I seem to have no control of, shines forth as spontaneous insights at the most unexpected times. Then they appear to leave as fast as they came, leaving only a trace of light in their passing.

John: You will see that the recognition continues to unfold naturally. This all gets introduced and you get a sense of what your real nature is. This was not clear previously. Still, the old ideas and habits to the contrary are in play. Often these arise in challenging situations or areas where we have invested a lot of our sense of identity. It could be work or relationships or whatever. But as the recognition of your true nature settles down, things resolve naturally. If you need guidance or some hands-on advice you can seek that out, like you are doing.

Q: Just now, as I was typing an inner voice asked, 'What is aware of the coming and going of insights?' Whose birthday?

John: Voila!

5

Trace the Root of Suffering

Question: I have enjoyed reading your articles, and things have begun to resonate. Reading them inspired me to purchase Bob Adamson's book and recently your own. If you do not mind, I wonder if you could help with the following. I find that when I am at home away from the routine of work and computers and there is no need to communicate and relate with people and friends, it is so much easier to become aware.

John: Well, if you look at this more finely, you discover that, as has been pointed out, awareness is ever-present. It does not become more present. As you begin to notice this fact, the wavering quality ends.

Q: At those times, I actually think, 'Hey, this is it. Yes, all is calm. The mind is quiet. I am aware, just aware. Oh, there goes a thought, oh, and another'. There is more silence and warm consciousness. I can almost see the 'I' thought fading away.

John: Just see that all these thoughts and experiences are appearing and disappearing in the undeniable awareness. It continues even when you are not thinking about it.

Q: As soon as I get back to work, the old conditioning just comes flooding back. I am that person again who needs to behave in the manner that others are used to.

John: These are just the old concepts. The main thing now is to see them as concepts. That is a good approach to getting some space around the experience.

Q: In those moments, it feels unnatural to be any other way.

John: You need to really see if the concepts are natural. In fact, they are highly artificial. They are conditioned ideas that we picked up in life before we knew any better.

Q: Sometimes I get very frustrated and instead of being relaxed and calm. I can display all kinds of behavioral patterns, from low moods, to sulking, to sudden desperation and anger towards others. I know people can also sense this. I think I am missing it somewhere and maybe even afraid of change. Although I somehow know life could flow so much more easily.

John: The real resolve on this is to trace the root of suffering and really see the mechanism of it. Otherwise, you are buffeted about without really having any solid ground to stand on. Here are some tips. Suffering is generated in the mind, in thinking. It does not exist anywhere else. The thoughts that create suffering are those that revolve around the sense of a separate self. This idea of being a limited separate being is the root driver of all self-centered experience. By inquiring into the validity of this core concept you can verify whether it is true or not. If it is seen to be false, then the basic cause is removed (through the seeing). This pulls the plug on the cause of suffering. The fact of present awareness that has been pointed out is seen to be simply the case. There is nothing to do or attain in terms of your true nature. Tackling the suffering through investigation has the effect of removing any camouflage from the clear and steady recognition of the ever-present and clear awareness. Still, regardless of what comes or not, or what is seen or not, you never move from your true nature.

Q: Any additional advice you can offer would be appreciated.

John: The bottom line is that this naturally becomes clear as the understanding settles in.

6

Do Not Fall for These Concepts!

Question: What you said last night about the 'mystery person' who attended your meeting struck a chord. He had been searching for decades and had only one question for you and then left, satisfied that his seeking was over. You said that his question was, 'What am I?'

John: It all boils down to that. That is why things do not feel complete and why the thought 'I am not there yet' still arises.

Q: You said something to me once about possibly needing something to latch onto before completely letting go of the false beliefs. I do not think I have a foothold yet on the foundation of what I am. I know the teaching—that I am awareness, consciousness, the supreme reality, cognizing emptiness—but I do not think I truly identify as that.

This is probably the 'stepless step' that only I can do, even though I am not doing any of this. Am I trying to reach for something that does not need to be grasped? Are you familiar with the position I am in? And then the question arises, 'Who is this "I" that needs to do something?'

If I am not that 'I' then what am I? I am present and aware. I am not a limited individual, nor am I the thoughts that arise, nor the mind from which they apparently arise. I am not anything that I can see or otherwise perceive. The thought that arises says, 'You cannot see the space, nor can you describe it, but you know it is there'. But I do not seem to be able to identify with—or as—nothingness.

The trick seems to be that I cannot get it with the mind,

but that I can possibly get it some other way. Then the thought arises that I should be able to realize it through direct experience. It is as though I need to disengage myself from this body and float out into the room and realize that I am still seeing and hearing everything. But that is not my direct experience, as I currently perceive it. I seem to be sitting here in a chair, striking this keyboard and writing this e-mail to you. So, what is the shift that needs to take place?

John: All I can say is—do not fall for these concepts!

Your experience and understanding are unfolding very nicely, and there is absolutely nothing wrong or missing! There is no one who needs to do anything, nor is there anything to be done—except to continue to see the false notions as false.

There is no need to identify with 'that' because you are that. You cannot really get it with the mind because the mind cannot get that which is prior to the mind. Nor can you get it through some other means because getting it implies that you haven't got it. But we are talking about your present awareness or sense of beingness, which is clear and undeniably here. So you can see that this is a useless conceptual loop based on some false premises.

There is no answer at the level you are trying to find it. It is a false dilemma. The best approach is to question the whole basis of the problem to see if it is true. It is a conceptual loop that will keep you spinning until you see it. Once you do, you will laugh! What are all these ideas and doubts arising in right now? As Bob Adamson says, 'What is wrong with right now, if you're not thinking about it?'

A shift implies getting something that is not present and that is presumed to exist in the future. Inquire into these concepts. If they are false, then the whole problem evaporates. Awareness is going on right now quite naturally. Things are being registered quite naturally. That is your direct experience. When your focus is not engaged in concepts generated in thinking, your experience is a natural peace and clarity. This is your direct experience. Do not discount your understanding or direct experience.

As you trust yourself and your direct experience more and more, all the steam goes out of taking the mind too seriously in these matters. You are left with simple presence-awareness, which is light and clear with no problems in sight. That is what you are.

Q: Thank you. Steady as s(he) goes!

The Ever-Present Obvious

Question: This morning I awoke, and there was boundless, spacious beingness. I was not identifying with anything solid. There were thoughts there, but they faded into the background. There was breathing, but I was even before that. There was stillness, and out of that stillness came movement. My leg, which was not even being perceived, moved and it temporarily brought me out of the feeling of pure beingness.

Then my eyes opened, and the world appeared, along with the body, and I began to connect myself with it. But there was a different flavor with that initially. It didn't seem real, not in an overwhelming sense, but much more subtle. Possibly with the comparison to what I now found to be real everything else lost its solidity. Again, it was very subtle. My senses seemed to be amplified, the opening of a door sounded like heavy metal on metal. I seemed to be watching the movements of the body, rather than causing them.

I know from reading some of your articles that other people experience the spaciousness, and then it apparently disappears (and you tell them that they cannot ever get out of awareness). But that is what happened to me. I lost it! The 'experience of being' seemed to last for just a few minutes, and I kept trying to recreate the 'space' I was in. But I could not reconnect with it. I have heard that if you get a glimpse of this it will continue to widen until it is the constant place in which you reside. Do you find that to be true?

John: What happens is that you begin to notice the ever-present awareness-presence that is being pointed out. It seems unfamiliar because we have not been paying attention to it.

In truth, it does not come and go and you do not lose it. It comes into view, seemingly momentarily, and then the focus goes back on the mind and the content of awareness because that is the habit. As you get familiar with this it seems to come to the forefront and become more clearly recognized. Even so, it is that simple and undeniable sense of beingness that is right with you. You are just becoming acquainted with the ever-present natural state. It is good that this is being recognized. It will come up and be seen more and more now that you have some sense of what is being pointed out.

It is actually where you are residing all the time. Do not interpret it in terms of an experience or event occurring in time. Events and time arise right within you. You just naturally settle in with the recognition of the ever-present obvious.

The 'I' that is trying to create an experience or reconnect with it is just an empty thought. That is the false idea of separation. Do not fall for it! You are the space in which thought arises. There is nothing to do or not do from this position. You are the space of presence. What does the space of presence need to do to connect with the space of presence? Just recognize what is already the case!

What Is Perception?

Question: What is perception?

John: The question can be tackled in different ways. Basically, a perception is just a movement in awareness. Upon investigation, you find that actually there is no independent object apart from the perception itself, nor is there any subject apart from the perception. The perception or act of perceiving, in turn, has no independent existence apart from awareness. So, even when seeming perceptions occur, all there is is just awareness or non-duality. That awareness or non-duality is your true nature. From this viewpoint, perception is really just another name for your own existence. Even in the midst of perceptions, you never move away from oneness. The same applies to the arising of thoughts, feelings, sensations and any other experiences.

All Fear Is Not Normal or Necessary

Question: Perception seems to arise only with the manifestation of a perceiver.

John: The perception or act of perceiving is factual. Both the object and subject are postulated. But your being and awareness are always there beyond doubt.

Q: It seems that attention can be moved around.

John: By whom? All the inquiries into the nature of perception are somewhat problematic, as they are conducted by the mind looking at the mind. It may be all right as philosophy, but the resolution of fear and suffering lies in self-knowledge or a direct, non-conceptual realization of awareness or being itself. It is not a thing that can be grasped, but it can be realized. The mind is completely useless for this!

Q: The brain seems quieter than ever. But there still arises the residue of fear.

John: What is the fear? Unless you are referring to some natural bodily or animal fear, the fear can usually be traced to a particular concept which we have identified with our sense of self. This can be resolved through clear seeing and understanding.

Q: When looked at, it tells me that there is something that needs attending to.

John: Yes, unless it is based on a faulty, erroneous concept. Then, it needs to be exposed and seen for what it is. Without any more specifics on this, it is hard to say. If the fear is based upon the belief in a separate self, then it is groundless. No amount of response to it would help much until the root is seen.

Q: It is almost like the brain demanding order. Awakening, if I may use that term, surely is not the end of past situations which have not been dealt with.

John: I have completely dropped the term 'awakening' from my vocabulary. There is no such thing. Time itself is a concept, so you need to be sure you do not give too much weight to where your mind is leading you on this one! As far as situations which have not been dealt with—by whom?

You see, as you start into these kinds of apparently simple discussions you can get into muddy water. A lot of the assumptions upon which the thinking is predicated turn out to be very doubtful. Instead of resolving the mind's dilemmas, it is more productive to question your premises.

Q: The right response seems to be the full-on doing of what needs doing as soon as possible.

John: I am not sure what you are referring to here.

Q: Fear is a useful warning system of present danger.

John: Sure, for real danger.

Q: If fear is arising it must be telling the system that something needs sorting out now.

John: Unless the fear is based on false premises. If you imagine a ghost in the closet, fear may arise. But it is not based on a valid cause. So all fear is not normal or necessary. If it is based on a faulty premise, it is better to get that resolved, rather than taking the fear to be legitimate and trying to respond to it.

Q: The following metaphor has been used: It seems like the motor has been switched off, but the fan blades are still turning. Gradually there seems to be less and less interest in this. However, I still feel the need to put some things right that can be put right.

John: This all sounds good. I am not really that keen on the revolving fan metaphor. Some people seem to use it to explain ongoing suffering that is not truly resolved. They have the idea that 'I am there' and explain away self-centered suffering as the winding down of the past momentum. That is all well and good if the basics are truly seen. A lot of times the root is not truly resolved and the explanation is just a gloss over the play of separation, which is in full swing. It takes a bit of honesty to look directly and see whether the belief in separation is in play. No amount of non-dual words will clear it up. But some sincere looking will.

In my experience, when the seeing of the non-existence of the separate 'I' registers, there is a decisive cutting of the root. There is not much room for having to deal with unresolved issues. Unresolved for whom? Questions themselves are an expression of the feeling that something is missing. Awareness does not need to answer any questions or resolve any issues. Still, if something comes up to act on or resolve, then that is the natural intelligence within you moving in that direction. Follow the promptings of your own heart and you cannot go wrong.

There Is No Need to Communicate with Awareness

Question: I have read and enjoyed your book 'Awakening to the Natural State'. It certainly confirms the state of crystal clear open clarity that I am. I also had the privilege to meet 'Sailor' Bob, as well as some other teachers of non-duality. It is truly wonderful how this simple message seems to be percolating into the play for so many characters and allowing a simple awakening to our natural state.

I have one simple question which I would like to hear an answer as you see it, given your own experience of this clarity. From the perspective of clear seeing, without any undue focus on passing mental content, awareness at any time is full of content, of whatever is arising in that moment. For me, the most intriguing aspect of all such appearance is what is seen as the light of awareness shining through the eyes of another human form. The challenge seems to be not to allow the story or mental content attached to that other apparent body to get in the way of the true seeing or communication with that shining awareness. That contact seems to me to be the essence of pure love, communion with your very own self appearing through the eyes of another body-mind, which of course can also even be an animal!

How do you see that communion? What does it mean for you? Even in silence with no need for words to be spoken, what is felt in that space of meeting oneself? How does that feel for you?

John: If you are the state of crystal clear open clarity, then what can I possibly say? Look into the eyes of any apparent other and see what comes up in your direct experience. Your answer is right there!

The whole thing about awareness and content is a little artificial, although it may be a useful teaching device. Is the content ever apart from awareness? Does it have any substance of its own? No! So there is no content, only awareness. That being so, there can be no distractions or challenges, because it is all oneness. There is no need to communicate with or see awareness, since you already are that. As long as bodies, minds and people are viewed as something apart, we will feel the need to resolve issues of communing and connecting. Transcend this concept by seeing that it is false and you will have no need to resolve the dilemma, because it is based on a false assumption. There is only one awareness. Know it as your true nature and all doubts are resolved.

Keep the Basics Clearly in View

Question: In your book you highlight to others two areas: 1) coming to see and recognize the clarity of the ever present-awareness, and 2) the seeing through or falling away of the sense of separation. I see the former clearly and without difficulty. It is the latter that still has a hold.

John: Often the dawning intuition of the positive nature of who and what we are seems to come more easily at first. It gets pointed out in no uncertain terms that what we are is the ever-present principle of being-awareness. Interestingly enough, even though it is absolutely clear and doubtless, it usually has been overlooked. The recognition is often immediate and obvious at the moment it gets pointed out.

But for many of us, the source of suffering, separation and confusion remains unresolved. I have covered this in other articles on my website. The mechanism of suffering is not yet clearly seen. However, once this gets clearly pointed out, there can be a direct seeing of this as well. Suffering ultimately lies in our own thoughts and nowhere else. The particular thoughts involved specifically are self-centered thoughts that revolve around who and what we imagine ourselves to be. These in turn are rooted in, or based upon, the fundamental concept of a separate 'I' or limited self, which we take to be present and which we mistake as who we are. All along, we are nothing but present awareness, and yet a conceptual confusion about our identity continues as long as it is not investigated. The investigation exposes the root of the error, and the cause is removed. This has the effect of pulling out the root driver of separation and suffering. The unity, which was never really lost, is restored. You are left in and as the natural state of simple being that was always the case. The life of individuality or the sense of being a separate self is really nothing more than a mistaken assumption. It is easily resolved through the application of a bit of clear seeing and investigation. It need not be a difficult or protracted affair if you keep the basics clearly in view.

Q: I can actually see that there is no separate self in the clear, knowing awareness that I know myself to be.

John: So far so good!

Q: Yet that sense of knowing seems to be so limited to a body's view of the world and feels separate from it.

John: Right now, awareness is taking in the whole of the manifestation. It is open, spacious and clear. It is not even really connected with the body, as the body is simply another object like so many others arising in awareness. This is the simple fact which is seen by just looking without giving any conceptual interpretation. Awareness cannot possibly be separate from the world because it is equally illuminating every bit of it. The whole of creation is just a movement in awareness. We do not even have any knowledge of the creation ever existing apart from awareness. So how can we speak of awareness as being separate from anything? Separation must be a concept, not a fact. We must question the concept before accepting it to be valid.

Q: But I have never known not seeing from this limited perspective.

John: I would instead point out that you have never been apart from that open and clear awareness, which is never separate from anything. You have never been out of that.

Q: Even if there is no real separation from this, the appearance of apparent others (also with knowing awareness) and how they react to and treat an apparent 'me' seems only to reinforce that sense of being separate from them and everything else. And this is the one thing I want—to be whole, not to be separate, to be one.

John: This is where the focus starts to go onto the belief that there is some substantial separate entity. The idea of separation is born only with the rise of this concept. Then all the trouble starts, all the questions begin, all the worries about others arise. If there is a separate 'I', then all these issues may be valid. But if you are not a separate being, but are really one with the principle of awareness, then the problem is solved because it has no basis. That is why I say do not try to resolve the problems but investigate the assumptions. Who and what am I? Have I ever, at any time, been separate from the principle of awareness or presence? If I think I am separate, can I find that supposed entity that I think I am? Where is it? How do I know it is there?

Q: Somehow, I need a different pointer to see past this blockage. Please help.

John: I sense you have a basic intuition that the 'I' as a substantial, independent entity may not be real or findable. Yet the old ways of thinking and viewing still continue through force of habit, causing you to take for granted that such an entity is there somewhere, however vaguely. Continue to probe into these matters and realize that the concept or belief in separation is the source of all problems and doubts. Investigate this until you are sure that you are—and can never be—anything else than the simple fact of present awareness. From this understanding, examine the beliefs and ideas in the mind and see how they are rooted in the belief in separation. You will

come to see that this idea is utterly unfounded. It is an imaginary concept arising and setting in the bright clarity of pure
awareness that you can never leave. Be willing to explore this
a bit and things will easily resolve into a direct knowing that
you never leave your true nature. All questions are resolved
because your nature is always oneness or non-duality.

You Are Always Home and Now You Know It

Question: The doubts are gone. No, the doubter is not arising and is nowhere to be found. What is interesting is that the observer has no independent existence. It arises with the observed. This seems to be the basic problem—we take the observer (watcher, seer, perceiver) to be real. The observer arises with the observed and sets with the observed. It is all within that which I have always been, ordinary presence-awareness. Another stumbling block is that there appears to be a perceiver of this presence of being. There isn't. Presence-awareness is all that is.

This invisible obviousness appears to have a shadow. We only have to switch on CNN to see what we, as this shadow, are doing. This shadow is the separation between the believer and the believed. The shadow is the known, and who I am is the unknown. It is pointless spending a lifetime trying to perfect, get rid of or enlighten the shadow. It is like seeing a lake in the desert and heading towards it for a drink. Someone along the way tells you it is a mirage. It can never be a lake again, although sometimes it appears to be. But now you know it is not and never has been. There is no need for any action. The action happened in the realization that it was a trick of the heat and light.

In 1986, Krishnamurti told me, 'The observer is the observed'. I quoted that for many years without having a clue about its real meaning. He also said, 'The first step is the last step'. All my paths have led towards that illusory lake in the desert. Sometimes I could have sworn I got my feet wet. That is what kept me going. John, there is only—thank you.

John: Good news. Glad to hear things have settled in and the mist that was never really there has departed! No matter what you think, say or do, you never leave the simple sense of presence-awareness, which is your real being. You are always home and now you know it. That is the greatest blessing.

Once You Have Seen This, There is No Going Back

Question: Sometimes there is clarity, a sense of endless, pure space that contains everything. At other times, there is complete involvement in 'me'. But there seems to be a growing sense of this 'me' as being empty of any substance. There is a great freedom and joy in realizing this. There is still a belief that some states are more 'it' than others, but I guess these all take place in awareness. Once it is realized that there is no separate 'me', is there any going back? Or is there a gradual unfolding of all this? It does feel like a door has been opened that was never closed (and in fact there never was a door).

John: Continue to investigate and lay bare the roots of suffering and separation. Trace them to the concept of a separate 'I'. Look at it every which way until you are convinced—by your own direct experience—that you have never been any such thing as an identifiable, separate entity. See that the roots of suffering lie in imagination only. Apply the basic pointers to your assumptions and beliefs. Through this, the ever-present clear being-awareness will be more and more certain.

Once you have truly seen all this for yourself, there is no going back. Mental insights or intuitions may come and go, but what is realized in direct knowing can never be lost.

Duality Never Happened

Question: Would you be so kind as to comment on the following? Presence-awareness manifests in a body complex ...

John: Not sure about this! Maybe the body manifests as an appearance in presence-awareness!

Q: How this happens I am not sure or whether it is important to know.

John: Who wants to know? The search for causes and reasons is definitely a pastime of the conceptual mind. Time, causation and reason are created in conceptual thought. Then the mind tries to understand the appearance in terms of the conceptual categories it has created. It is a false endeavor, really.

Q: The presence and that from which it arises are one and the same.

John: Yes. So, ultimately, any question is based on the notion of separation, which never really happened. So the question is really insoluble in thought. It is a false question. When you see that the question is false, you do not solve it, you discard it.

Q: That which always is has not changed in any way.

John: True.

Q: Awareness is misidentified as a cognizer. I have not looked into how this could happen.

John: At the level of awareness, there is only oneness. It is all awareness, so what is to identify with what? Be careful of your premises. Search for the one that is seemingly misidentified and you find it is not there!

What you find is that the question of when, why and how awareness got misidentified is a false problem. The problem is not solved, it is dismantled. It is like asking: When, where and how was the man-in-the-moon born? He wasn't. You just see the falseness of the question. The question assumes that something happened—but it didn't. Awareness has never been limited, confined or misidentified.

Q: The cognizer is mistaken to be the subject 'I' (the individual), but it is not a subject. It is an object. There is not a person and never has there been.

John: That sounds good, especially the last statement.

Q: From there, everything that arises in the mind as an object is seen by the cognizer (masquerading as subject) as an object separate from itself. Really, this is an object appearing in consciousness as consciousness. Everything arises in awareness as (object) consciousness. There is just awareness and what we could term objects arising and setting in awareness.

John: Seemingly. But this is a provisional point of view. Because objects arise and set in awareness and have no independent existence apart from awareness, they are only that. There is no division, just like with waves and the sea. We imagine separation then go about trying to explain the reason for the separation. But if there is no separation to begin with, there is no need to explain it!

Q: Ignorance begins when the cognizer identifies itself as subject.

John: Not really. There is no such thing as a cognizer. That in itself is a makeshift concept for communication purposes.

Q: The cognizer and the cognized are one and the same.

John: The cognizing is real, but the cognized and cognizer are assumed. Show me any such thing as a cognizer or any object existing independently of being cognized. In one sense they are the same—they are both imaginary concepts.

Q: In reality there is no such cognizer and cognized. Only all-knowing presence-awareness.

John: Yes, you have said it now. The need to explain and analyze is a remnant habit of thought. All I can say is that if you are going to do it, do it clearly and accurately. Most importantly, lay bare the assumptions that generate false problems.

I would be wary of trying to pin all this down in a 'proper conceptual model'. Awareness is here. It is doubtless. It has no questions at all. By definition, all questions must be appearances in thought. What is a question but a thought? Awareness knows thoughts, but thoughts can never know awareness. When you see this, the energy goes out of trying to solve riddles in thought. When the clarity, peace and unshakable certainty of being is evident, trying to solve questions is not really needed!

Questions ultimately boil down to the following. There is something I need to know, something that I am missing. If I had the answer, I would be more certain, more happy, more complete. But when the answer is your own ever-present being, where is the need to ask anything? That is at the highest level of looking at this. In awareness, as it is, there are no others, no appearances, no time, no space, no thought, no doubt, nothing to understand. All appearances are just a movement in awareness. They have no real being. So all there is, is that.

Under no circumstance do you leave your real nature. Ultimately, nothing needs to be explained because duality never really happened. There was never an object or a subject, nor was there anyone misidentified. All apparent problems stem from the apparent non-recognition of present awareness. Yet even that never happened!

Awareness Is Not a Realization

Question: This morning the thought came to me that 'I' could expand my perception of myself as awareness.

John: Is there any 'I' to do anything? Awareness is here. You are that. Who needs to do something? Be careful of falling into false concepts!

Q: Bob Adamson once said something to me about how I was able to hear a noise out on the street because I was out 'there' as well. This morning, I could hear the garbage trucks passing by, and at the same time I could hear and feel my breathing. I was also aware of the thoughts passing by. All was present in the awareness that I am. I finally had a glimpse of something that has escaped me—that there is no 'in' or 'out'.

John: Good! Everything is in awareness. 'In' and 'out' are conceptual labels, not given in direct experience.

Q: Also this morning, I was washing my face and began to just experience the foamy feeling of the soap, the pressure of my fingers on my skin and the scent of the soap. For a moment there was only the experiencing of it without 'me' being there. It was strange focusing on that as it happened. I realize that the same thing happens every morning, but I am lost in thought about what needs to be done at the office or whatever. But in this case the focus was on the actuality of what is, and at that moment I was not thinking I was a person. I was just experiencing.

John: That is what is going on all the time. It is not a realization or attainment, just the natural state of affairs, when conceptual thought is not being overlaid on experience.

Q: I do not know if I have reported this to you before, but sometimes after having a realization come up, I get a queasy stomach.

John: Awareness is not a realization. It is an ever-present fact. Queasiness or no queasiness, awareness is there straight through registering everything. There is no such thing as realization or awakening, just discovering what is right here. Being so clear and present, we overlook it and imagine realizations.

Q: I imagine you would say, 'Who gets a queasy stomach?'

John: No, you said it!

Q: Well, I guess I need to keep looking into that.

John: When the separate 'I' is completely dismantled and seen to be not present, the doubts and questions are no more.

Q: I also have to report that anxiety still rears its ugly head. It comes in waves, and I deal with it in the moment, but sometimes it can get overwhelming.

John: Continue to lay bare and expose the roots of suffering.

Q: Am I imagining things? I just had this insight that what I am does not move. I do not go anywhere. Everything 'out there' is just an illusion. When I grasp for something and feel the solidness or texture of it that itself is part of the illusion. Do I exist in my own private world? But then what about you and everyone else? Is this what is meant by I am alone (all one)? Who is everyone?

John: There is simply non-duality or oneness. There is nothing other than this. You are this. All is this. Separation is only imagined and assumed. All there is, is oneness. It is not alone, because being alone really implies that I am separate and alone in relation to something else. This oneness beyond words is light, love, presence, joy without words, divinity, peace, reality. Whatever you call it, you are that.

All Teachings Are Provisional

Question: On your website, you encourage one questioner to 'examine the beliefs and ideas in the mind and see how they are rooted in this idea of separation'. How does one actually do this? I can see that I am present awareness and that the world is not separate from awareness. I see that the body arises as an appearance in present awareness. I can see (when I am not mucking around in the story!) that thoughts, sensations and emotions arise in awareness. But the 'psychological sense of self' and how you investigate the falseness of that is not clear. It is the last little bit. You said to 'investigate until you have no doubts that you are—and can never be—anything else than the simple fact of present awareness'. It seems that it is already seen, and yet ... !

John: The 'and yet' is really just a symbol for any lingering doubts or questions of separation or any residual belief that there is something other than present, already realized awareness. What I find in speaking with others is that nothing new is really brought in at this point, but through dialogue and looking for oneself, the contrary concepts get dismantled.

There are actually different ways to approach this. They are all relative and really designed to dismantle the particular questions and doubts. You can take the approach that everything is the perfection and there is nothing to do. You can take the approach that awareness is like an unstained mirror and that no matter what comes up, it (you) remains unaffected. Or you can dismantle the thoughts and concepts through investigation to see if their source or basis is true. You can take the approach that everything is God's will, so why worry about anything? There are probably many more. However, none of these pointers themselves is the actual understanding, the direct, non-conceptual knowing of your own real being. All teachings are relative and provisional. As Nisargadatta Maharaj might say, the purpose is simply to liquidate the questioner or to eliminate the separate person as a factor in consciousness.

My own pointers, by necessity, come out in a specific way, which is largely based on how I saw this and what worked for me. It is inevitable that people tend to communicate this in a manner that worked for them. It is often based on how their teacher (if they had one) pointed things out. Every expression is a little different and does not necessarily 'click' for everyone. There is no one-size-fits-all answer, because everyone's doubts and questions are somewhat unique. That is why one-on-one dialogue and personal interaction is often helpful if there are any lingering doubts.

When I say investigate the person and its stories, it presupposes some intuition or sense of your real nature as undeniable, present awareness. Just see clearly that this is what is being pointed out. It is that natural and easily recognized sense of being aware, being present. There is really nothing more to know or understand. Resting in and as that, which you already are, you are home. All suffering or problems at that point, if any arise, are just movements in thought. And you, in fact, never move at all from presence or the natural state. Sometimes, this seeing is enough in itself. This insight was hugely impactful for me. When I saw this, it ended once and for good the notion that we go in and out of clarity. But still the question of why the troubling thoughts arise may come up. You see that all such thoughts are based upon a sense of 'me', some deficient, imperfect person. You can look at your own troubling thoughts and concepts to see if this is true or not. Do not take my or somebody else's words to be true, but look for yourself and see if you can see if this is the case or not.

All the conceptual thoughts revolve around a limited, defective sense of 'me' that the mind takes to be real. Even when there has been some clear seeing that the 'I' is absent, the mind continues, out of habit, to work under the assumption that it is present. But you can start to investigate this and question it a bit. You can look for any independently existing person and see if you can find any such thing at all. There is existence. There is awareness. There are a handful of thoughts, perceptions, and feelings arising in the moment—but that is all. All else is imagination, that is to say, it is not really present, except as a concept. 'Time', 'space', 'causality', 'me', 'you', 'good', 'bad', 'liberation', 'bondage'—all of these are imaginary concepts. They are just words! None of them are given in direct experience.

Seeing that there is no separate person is something you can see for yourself by looking and investigating. Where is the separate, defective person? Have you ever seen any such thing? The mind may continue with this belief out of habit, but you have seen the true position. There has never been any separate or substantial entity or person at all. But you cannot deny the fact of your own real being, which is clearly present and brightly aware. That awareness is not a thought, an experience, or imagined person. It is the clear, open light of knowingness, which is like a mirror in which everything is spontaneously reflected. Yet it is completely clear and untouched.

All this is seen and looked into. It is easy and natural because it is going on all the time without effort. This seeing naturally dismantles all doubts, beliefs and feelings of separation. Even if they come up, the realization of the ever-present clarity is so evident and compelling that no energy or attention goes into conceptual thought any longer. Even if it does, it does not really matter because you can never get out of the fact of your own being. This all becomes clear naturally. Once the seed is planted, the flower comes forth.

There is No 'You' Doing Anything

Question: At your job, you do things all the time. It is you who are doing the doing, and it is you whom your colleagues acknowledge, right? Are you saying you just witness yourself doing while maintaining the state of integration? You act but are not of the action?

John: The short answer is that there is no 'me' or 'you' doing anything. It is all just a spontaneous happening or functioning. The idea of 'you' is a learned concept. There is no need for integration, because there is no 'you' who needs to be integrated. Awareness is. You are that. The only problem is that this has been overlooked and we have imagined separation, individuality, and doer-ship—none of which is true. Clearing up that misunderstanding is the aim of inquiry.

There is thinking, but no one thinking. There is action but no one acting. There are decisions, but no one deciding. This is happening for you right now. All doer-ship is completely imagined—and yet all doing goes on just fine. It is just like your heart is beating, your blood is circulating, your organs are functioning quite well, but there is no 'you' doing any of it. The thinking is also happening just fine, but there is no 'you' doing that either.

Discovering that there is no separate 'you' means the root of all problems is resolved. All problems are for 'someone'— and there isn't one. So the game is up. Suffering and doubts come to an end. The illusion is removed, and life goes on in freedom. This is the natural state.

Has Your True Nature Gone Anywhere?

Question: I just wanted to touch base with you and see if you might have a suggestion on my current position, or if you could at least relate to it. As I mentioned in my last e-mail, while driving home from the airport there was an experience like I had never had. The manifested simply went away (including me). Literally none of the physical experience existed. The background of abundant, complete and whole emptiness was in clear view. It was obviously the real! It was full of peace and love. I knew beyond any conscious knowing what home was and what would be present after the body-mind is gone. There was no individual existence (as we know it through separation), but just the one which I am. Peace and love had new meaning that cannot be expressed. The pointers I have read and heard about took on a whole new meaning.

John: This is a wonderful insight. But do not focus on it as an experience or something that occurred at a point in time. Rather, see that you were actually noticing the ever-present background. If viewed as an experience, the mind will want to repeat it or try to project the knowing of what is real as an event. Then several false concepts come back into play: 1) that there is an individual who is waiting for something, 2) that time is real, 3) that understanding will come in the future, and 4) that the real is an experience, rather than the constantly present background of all experiences. All of these are subtle concepts that divert the attention away from the recognition of what is present and already the case.

Q: The presence-awareness we speak of was there, but it was magnified a thousand-fold and at the same time within the one wholeness. Nothing could be wrong, and it was obvious that nothing has ever happened. As the manifest returned, it first appeared superficial and laughable, as if a child had attempted to create it out of modeling clay. It appeared fragile and superficial. The manifest was not even close to what was real. Then the manifest took on an assumed reality again, and the experience was over.

John: That is a good seeing, and it aligns with the true state of affairs. But it is not an experience or event. It is just the way things are. The old concepts tend to perpetuate the idea that this is some rare state that special beings attain or that we will attain if we are lucky. But this idea blocks the immediate recognition that what was seen was simply the way things are. The recognition of your true nature as presence-awareness allows the seeing of the real nature of the appearance. All things are just movements of energy within the ever-present clarity. It is not really true that presence-awareness gets magnified a thousand-fold. It may appear that way when some of the old concepts drop out of the picture. But can you say the awareness is more or less aware, or that existence is more or less existent?

Q: Since that time, my experience has been like being in the desert.

John: You may not be having the rapturous mystical experience or the radical dropping away of the appearance. But has your true nature actually gone anywhere? Use this experience as a way to see that the understanding of who you are is not about some particular, wonderful state of affairs within the appearance. Perhaps there is some remnant belief hanging in there that self-knowledge implies some fantastic shift in the manifestation. But the appearances are just temporary and constantly change. If you are looking for some special configuration to arise within the appearance, you will be disappointed. The key is to understand what is ever-present and constantly with you. Take your stand there, and then the appearances are irrelevant. Even in the experience of being 'in the desert' you must be present and aware. Your identity as the presence-awareness is what is to be understood.

Q: That knowing and oneness is now only a memory.

John: Again, use this as a means to a deeper understanding. Is your true being a memory? See that you are not a memory, nor is the recognition of your real nature connected with memory. Memories are just ideas. They are appearing right within what is present and aware. If we are looking into experiences and time, we are looking away from the essence.

Q: There is an apparent slow death of the person and the sense of a homecoming, while at the same time there is obviously some clinging to the thoughts.

John: There are still some habits and concepts coming up that are believed to some extent. That is all. There cannot really be a slow death of a person, because there is no person. It is like saying that the man-in-the-moon is slowly disappearing. The most direct course is just to get the old concepts out on the table for inspection and investigation. Seeing the false as false leaves you with what is true.

Q: There is an attempt to keep coming back to the presence-awareness, but it is as if that is done, like it is time to leave that boat at the edge of the river.

John: Who is going to leave that, and where is he going to go? You cannot get away from the essential understanding, which is that your nature is that which is present and aware. You have never been apart from that, and that is all there is. There is nothing really more to see beyond that.

Q: I know you will probably suggest just staying with the presence-awareness—and I am. But where it used to 'snap' and bring things into perspective or into the real, now there is no event.

John: It is good to see that! Question whether or not this is about experiencing some event. It is this concept that is the problem, not the simple recognition of your nature as presence-awareness. The subtle expectation of some freeing event diverts the attention from seeing what is here. Then if the expected event does not manifest, we are disappointed. But it is the conceptual assumptions that generate this experience. All the while, your true nature shines clear and bright, illuminating all of these thoughts and experiences.

Q: I do not know how to express this, except that the mind is still longing. That wholeness is obscured. The tools for apparent progress are failing to finish their job. The experience described above has become somewhat of an expectation for the future, which is obviously part of the problem.

John: Come back to the basics, as you are doing. Question the assumptions that are coming up due to the old habits. Is your nature something that will appear in the future? If not, why wait around for some imagined event? Do you need a set of tools to recognize the fact of your own being?

At this point, there is really nothing to do because you already have a strong recognition of your real nature. You are just getting bamboozled by a few old concepts that tend to pull you away from simply acknowledging and resting in what is clear, present and obvious. So, as I mentioned before, just get these old ideas out for inspection and question them. In seeing them to be false, you have no other place to be but with what is present. The concepts have the effect of acting as a veil or obscuration—until they are seen. However, past a point you realize that even the concepts are appearing and disappearing right in the clarity you are seeking. Then you see that you never leave that. You cannot get away from what you are.

Q: The mind cannot get there or go there, but it is hanging on to the idea nonetheless. While I see all of this as events within awareness, there is an expectation that there should come a 'break' where the manifestation falls clearly into its proper place and being-ness takes center stage.

John: But this is wrong. There is no need for some break or change in the manifestation. Can you really say that the present beingness is not already in its proper place? Isn't being-awareness already at center stage, making all appearances possible? Again, there is a subtle concept in play that the reality is not present, so the mind starts to look into time and events, wondering 'When will it happen?'

Q: As I re-read this, I see the holes, and I know what I would say if I were receiving this e-mail from someone else. I believe (even though I cannot trust the concept) that I am standing on the edge, just waiting to be pushed off forever, but still clinging to the thought of 'getting it'.

John: The best approach is to see if the notion that you are an entity 'standing on the edge' (of reality, I presume?) is true. Who is this 'I' standing on the edge? At this moment, can you really find any such thing? If there is no separate entity, who is on the edge? Who needs to get something? Is there anything wrong with presence-awareness? Are you something apart from that?

Q: The one believing this obviously cannot take the step off the edge, cannot get it or do anything else.

John: Yes, because he does not exist. See that you have never been any kind of an entity apart from the real, and all the questions and problems are resolved once and for good. The imagined separate seeker does not exist. You are, and always have been, the reality you are seeking.

Q: Thank you for your response. It is greatly appreciated. After reading it several times, the foundation is under my feet again.

19

Loneliness Arises Through Belief in Separation

Question: I like to shift into being the awareness only. It is the only relief I get from the human condition, which seems brutal, even among friends.

John: Well, this is not a matter of shifting, much less a matter of 'you' doing something. In this approach, it is simply pointed out that you are always that. Full stop. It is recognized. That is all.

If you are talking about suffering, suffering is subjective and caused by our own concepts and beliefs. The externals, including other people, are just fine, as is.

Q: The problem is that I am alone.

John: Loneliness is one of those self-centered states that arises with the concept of being separate. Once this erroneous idea is seen through, you are not plagued by these kinds of things. In the ultimate sense you are alone, because you are the sole reality. But that is also the source of peace and love, so there is not a sense of loneliness. Loneliness arises through belief in separation.

Q: When trying to find others to show them how to be awareness only, I run into problems.

John: There are no others. Everything is just an expression of the underlying oneness. Sometimes it comes up to share; other times not. Only the separate 'I' has problems. Take care of that and everything will fall into place. There is no need to show people how to be awareness. They are awareness. No techniques are needed. If anyone is interested, you can just point back to the basic facts. There is no need to seek out converts! Also, you cannot really help others until you are beyond the need of help yourself.

Q: Some will even say that I am evil.

John: 'I', 'others', 'evil' and so on are just concepts! See your true nature and you will not be bothered by any concepts, not even your own.

Q: I like to use some of the Douglas Harding tools, such as watching the scenery move past me while walking (as if I am still). That shifts the mind into noticing awareness (awareness without me).

John: These are good pointers, but you can move beyond the need for any tools and just recognize that awareness is your ever-present true nature. This is the natural state.

Q: When trying to be with other humans in the human condition, I do not fit, from the position of being awareness only.

John: You seem to have some misunderstandings about this. There is no 'I' and nothing that needs to be done. It is only the 'I' that feels like it fits or not. If the 'I' is not real, then all of these problems are resolved.

Q: People pull me back into being the human identity instead of being awareness only.

John: No, this is not possible. It is our own ideas, beliefs and concepts that obscure things. See through those first, then everything takes care of itself. You can never be pulled out of your real state, because you are never separate from your true nature. Nothing and no one can ever pull you out of this.

Q: As awareness are we destined to be alone? Is there something to do and, if so, how to find out what that something is?

John: We have taken ourselves to be something we are not and suffer. Once we see that we have never been a separate person or 'I', all the problems and questions are solved. As I say elsewhere on my website:

> 'You are not the limited person you have taken yourself to be. Look for the separate self and you find it entirely absent. Seeing this, suffering, doubt and confusion effortlessly drop away, revealing your natural state of innate happiness and freedom'.

It may be good to talk to someone about this in person if the basics are not clear.

My sense is that you have some good insights but are not yet clear on the fundamentals, such as what is the root cause and cure of suffering. This is rarely communicated clearly by teachers (that I am aware of).

20

The Maintenance-Free Natural State

Question: In one of your recent e-mails you wrote 'Just continue to probe into this until it is clear and solid for you'.

John: I still stand by that!

Q: What I am trying to see right now is how to probe into it without getting the mind involved.

John: As you sense, it is best not to run this through the mind. The mind or thinking process is not the best tool for this. The mind thinks thoughts. It can view and deal with thoughts. But your real being (awareness) is not a thought. So if you look with mind, you will miss it. However, you do not really have to look for it because it is right with you. It is the undeniable sense of presence, awareness or being (or whatever we want to call it) that is the background of all appearances. It is absolutely and fully present and clear right now.

Q: The presence, while pervasive enough, is so subtle and in the background!

John: Awareness seems subtle because we have been focusing on appearances in the awareness. Once you start to take note of your real nature, there is a deepening recognition of it. As you stay with the noticing of this, you begin to discover its qualities more and more. It is not an effortful process. It is just getting acquainted with something we have overlooked.

Q: I keep thinking that I need to do something to bring it more to the forefront.

John: There is no 'I' who needs to do anything! Do not turn this into a project for the person who thinks he is not there yet. Just let the pointers resonate and follow them out of a natural sense of curiosity.

Q: Needless to say, trying to do something does not work. Then the mind starts up with the old 'maybe I do not really see it after all', and I see how counterproductive the whole 'doing' thing can be.

John: Good seeing! That is just spinning in needless conceptual thought. Just see it for what it is and that approach falls away naturally.

Q: But if I do nothing, it seems to get shoved into the background of work, kids, thinking and so on. That does not seem right either.

John: If you want to get to the heart of this really look into the sense of 'I' that thinks it can do or not do something. Is that real? Does awareness ever really get shoved into the background? Isn't it always present illuminating everything? There is no need to maintain anything. Once the awareness is pointed out, there is just a natural recognition that comes up.

Q: Interestingly enough, I had the exact opposite reaction from you about meditation, in that I am drawn to meditation more than usual, just because it seems easier to stay with presence at those times.

John: If that works, then go for it! Whatever you do, continue to look deeply into whether or not awareness is something you are ever apart from. What is your relationship with awareness? And who is the one who feels he can get away from it? Resolve these questions and you are left with a direct recognition of the maintenance-free natural state.

21

You Never Leave 'OK'

Question: This evening while driving home I was passing the time settling in with presence. Then I began doing what Nisargadatta Maharaj refers to as tracing the source of the 'I'. I always ended up empty handed whenever I tried to find the source. There it finally was. Why does this have to be so simple! The thought 'I' was nothing more than a reference or pointer back to that presence-awareness. It is the label that the mind has given to the presence-awareness, which the mind knows is there but cannot claim for itself. 'I' is the mind's way of referring to that. The 'I' does not refer to a person at all but to that which cannot be known by the mind. A few miles later the question arose, 'What do 'I' know about this presence?' Then the loop was seen. The thought 'I', which is nothing but a reference or pointer to the presence, was supposedly asking what it knows about presence. The loop is—you are what you seek.

I never really understood the notion that the 'I' cannot do anything. It seemed like it was doing a lot! But when it is seen that the 'I' is just a pointer to the presence-awareness, how can that pointer be doing anything?

John: Thanks for sharing your insights. It appears like the wide open highways of Oklahoma have been your natural meditation hall. Just remember that wherever you go, you never leave 'OK'!

Yes, the 'I' cannot ever do anything because it is just a concept. It has no substance or reality. It only points to the always attained reality of presence-awareness that you never leave. So, what is to be done when you are already that?

The seeming separate 'I' that we took ourselves to be was never really present. All questions, doubts, doings and not doings were based on the apparent separate 'I'. When that is seen to be absent, except as an imagined concept, the rug is pulled out from under the whole production. With no 'I', who has a problem? Who needs to do anything? Who needs to attain anything? You are simply as you have always been. The basis of the problem has been resolved through clear seeing.

~ Follow up ~

Q: I just wanted to touch base with you and to thank you for ending a twenty-five year search. It is done, over, no more. What else can be said?

The Normal State

Question: It is really utterly simple, isn't it? There is no one. That is it. Whatever this is, it contains everything. All striving, seeking, sense of separation—these are all it, too. And it all arises for no one. It is just a continuous arising for no one. It is too simple, but ever so clear. Everything is seen as it is without someone to sort it, claim it or judge it. It is just as it is. It is OK and needs nothing. (I cannot really do it justice in words.) In another way, nothing has changed. Thank you for your clarity.

John: Thank you for sharing your comments. The simplicity of all this is really the key. What you are seeing sounds excellent. The most direct confirmation of this is your own experience. When you see how direct and simple it is, the doubts, questions and problems get undercut at the source. The recognition of the clear, present awareness is utterly beyond doubt. Nothing necessarily changes in the appearance of living, but things are no longer being filtered through a screen of unexamined beliefs and reference points. The core unexamined concept is the belief in a separate someone at the center of experience. All other concepts hang on that one. When it is seen (not by an individual!) that the individual is absent, all the questions fall to pieces and life in clarity remains. It is utterly simple, utterly clear, utterly profound—and utterly normal. The natural state could also be called the normal state!

Everything Takes Place In Empty Awareness

Question: I had the insight today that during the course of the day the mind frequently jumps to another topic, like flipping TV channels. But the experience also occurred that my mind jumped to 'no thought', or to empty awareness. And there was the realization that that is really all there is to it!

John: No matter where the mind is jumping to, it is all taking place right within empty awareness. That is all there is to it. And you are that. You have always been that. So this has the effect of bringing the seeking and questions to a halt because you are already that. It was so simple that we overlooked it. Now you know the open secret. No matter what the mind thinks or does not think, everything takes place right within the space of empty, clear presence-awareness. That is the essence in a nutshell.

Do Not Wait for the Penny to Drop!

Question: I know that there is no me, no mind and even my thoughts are not my own. However, this understanding seems intellectual. There has not been the realization of this. The penny has not dropped.

John: The simplicity of this is often overlooked, and then the mind tries to come up with some explanation for why the understanding has not 'happened'. But it is not really like this. Your sense of existence and awareness is clear and well known now—not intellectually, just in direct experience. That simple sense of presence-awareness is all that is being pointed to. As the focus settles into this, everything becomes clear.

The whole notion of waiting for the penny to drop is a concept based on the subtle notion that what you are is not here, that it is not attained. Rather than waiting for the penny to drop—and it will never drop because your own being is not a future event—it is better to revisit the basics to see that the essential pointers are really clear.

Q: Having been on the spiritual path for nearly thirty years, and being a disciple of two 'masters' now dead, the last two years I have been on an intensified search. Fortunately, this has veered to the Advaita world—Ramesh Balsekar, Nisargadatta Maharaj, Tony Parsons and finally to the simplicity of 'Sailor' Bob Adamson. I picked up your book from 'Sailor' Bob. There is a resonance in your book that prompts me to ask you if you can point to something that may help the penny to drop.

John: Give up the idea of waiting for the penny to drop! This is 'barking up the wrong tree'. He who waits, waits forever. So there must be something unclear in the question or the approach. There is never anything attained, because you are—and always have been—what you are seeking. However, the subtle wrong assumptions and beliefs can be exposed through investigation. Then you are left with what I call 'the ever-present obvious'.

The simple fact of being and awareness, which is fully present and fully clear for you right now, is all that is being pointed out. Everything else is a concept. And those concepts are arising right here in the awareness itself. The awareness that you are is illuminating all doubts and questions. We have been looking for something else, yet the answer is the doubt-less fact of awareness, which is illuminating the (apparent) seeker's thoughts, even now. Watch how much of the mind's activity is based on beliefs contrary to this. The mind runs in grooves based on the notion that you are something limited. Just see that more clearly. The seeing itself is enough to break up the belief in the contrary concepts.

25

That in Which Thought Arises and Sets

Question: Currently, I am just going along reading spiritual materials, listening to CDs, and seemingly waking up over and over again to a present awareness that seems to be lost over and over again.

John: But is your actual being and awareness ever lost? Do you need to wake up to it over and over again? Or is it just a simple ever-present fact? In truth, it is never lost because it is the necessary background for all possible experiences and non-experiences. It is there without change throughout waking, dreaming and dreamless sleep. It is that simple sense of presence which is constantly there and within which everything appears.

Q: Only a few times has this awareness been what I might call deep. Usually, it is just a waking to simply look at what is here before me. But that is followed by a sense of losing it again.

John: Do not look at the content of awareness, which is variable. Look to that in which thoughts arise and set. It is neither deep nor shallow. Experiences come and go, but awareness itself is never lost. It is always right here with you. It is you. Until the simplicity of this is recognized, we pursue it (awareness) as if it is something apart and distant from us. There is no realizing of awareness. It is just a pointing to a simple yet often overlooked fact going on right now.

Q: I am so much more peaceful and happy than a few months ago, and conditions in all areas of my life have improved immensely without 'me' doing anything at all.

John: There has never been a 'me'. This is simply discovered, gradually or suddenly. All problems hinge on the assumed presence of a 'me'. Without that concept dominating thinking, there is just the natural state of simple freedom and clarity. It naturally begins to shine through life more and more, like the rising of the sun at dawn.

26

Your Own Being Is the Heart of the Matter

Question: I have gradually been realizing that this is too simple! At the moment even the idea of reading a book about this seems a little ridiculous. However, when it seems like it is something that is not already here, I find your book very helpful and reassuring, and it helps me identify what it is that I am getting hung up on that makes it appear so. One thing I have noticed that has changed, though, is that even though it resonated with me when I first read it, I wanted to keep reading more (like an insatiable appetite for knowledge). Now, I only read a section or two, which helps me get clear on the basics again, and then I put the book aside.

It appears that the sense of presence comes and goes. But it has been sinking in that the sense of presence is what underlies everything in my experience, so I know that it cannot really come and go. When it seems like it is here, I do not need anything. For a long time, I really could not quite understand what you and Bob Adamson were talking about when saying the idea of a separate person was false. Recently, the two fundamental points that you really helped clear up for me have blended synergistically. First, presence-awareness is all there is. Therefore, any apparent self (little 's') is just a passing thought, experience or happening in awareness. Second, Bob Adamson's often repeated saying that the separate self has no independent nature finally rings a bell without initiating a flurry of questions.

Your book and Bob's books and recordings have been the closest thing for me to a 'satsang' or attending your talks. I am starting to feel like this might really be the end (of seeking) and the beginning of just being. I actually feel a little giddy and a little disoriented at the same time right now. Probably the best description of what I started experiencing very subtly a couple days ago and more strongly today is the sense of 'un-caused joy', as Bob describes it.

I still sense that I am not totally clear on differentiating my experience or how I feel from just being-knowing what I really am, but I know something is happening. Or maybe to say it another way, I am getting clearer about what is real.

I will take your advice and just try to relax with it without analyzing it. I really appreciate your generosity in sharing your experience in all of this and spending the time to help me and others. I will keep in touch.

John: All this sounds excellent. From what you are saying, things are unfolding naturally and the various pointers are striking home more and more clearly. Your use of the books and pointers is fine, because you are using them for the time being to bring you back to looking at your direct experience. As long as that is the focus, reading about this and listening to talks on CDs or whatever can be helpful reminders.

The sense of joy is a good sign. This is because knowledge of our true nature and happiness always go hand in hand. If you are investigating all this but there is no joy or peace, the looking is probably coming in at a mental level. That is use-ful as a sanity check on how all this is striking home and how clearly you are understanding things.

Notice that feelings, just like thoughts and perceptions, arise in awareness. Feelings are passing objects or states that appear in the steady and clear awareness. Whether you are feeling so-called positive or negative feelings something must be there registering them. That steady and undeniable pres-ence is what is being pointed to.

I am glad to hear that things are resonating. That is the deeper truth within you resonating with the pointers. The pointers are secondary. What is being pointed to is your own real being. That is the heart of the matter. That is something right with you all the time. Once that is pointed out and you get a feel for it, you can just relax into that. Everything unfolds from the non-conceptual recognition of your true nature of being-awareness.

27

The Source of Happiness Is Within You

Question: I am starting to see that the joy or pure happiness is a powerful indicator for me. It has seemed to me that when I notice that that is missing I have a tendency to start looking in the mind to see what is wrong or what happened to it. But perhaps it is the other way around—I have drifted back to the mental perspective already.

John: You are starting to see this. Do not leave it at 'perhaps'. Investigate this until you see the truth of what is going on. Then the understanding is yours.

Q: I woke up today feeling like it was gone or at least greatly diminished, but just by relaxing into this anyway, the clarity and joy is becoming more apparent again.

John: It is always there. When the attention wanders into concepts and thoughts, the ever-present joy seems to fall to the background. Our habit has been look to thoughts for happiness. It is just a basic ignorance about the source of happiness. But then you discover that the actual source of happiness is within you. Very naturally, the attention ceases to run into thoughts and concepts. You just remain easily in your natural state of relaxed freedom.

It is not so much about doing as it is about clear understanding. There is not much more to it than that. Once the basics are seen, things fall into place quite naturally.

Q: There is also still a sense of 'Is this for real?' 'Is this really it?' 'Am I deluding myself?' and so on. I guess one 'answer' to that is 'Who cares?' or 'Who wants to know?'

John: See that these are all thoughts—just thoughts and nothing else. They arise and set right in the space of clear, open awareness. The answer was so simple, we overlooked it. But from now on, you can no longer say that you do not know. Old habits may surface, but they are seen and they drop away in the seeing. Whether they appear or not is ultimately immaterial because everything is always taking place right in present awareness. In this approach, the separate 'I' and all the false concepts are checkmated once and for all.

28

Separation Has Never Occurred

Question: I am still working with things, but you have pointed me back to the obvious.

John: It all comes down to that. Your existence, which is also aware, is here in all its fullness. We just did not think there was anything interesting about it! It turns out to be the master key. Getting this pointed out in no uncertain terms is an essential turning point. From then on, you cannot go back. No matter how much the mind jumps around and tries to search for answers elsewhere, the essential pointing has struck home. What you are seeking you already are. This is the essential message.

Q: Yet there is still something that seems elusive about it!

John: Right now, right here, is the fact of being-awareness elusive, mysterious or unknown in any way, shape or form? The whole answer is here, shining in plain view.

Q: At this point, I am just trying to really understand that it is all just awareness and I am that.

John: This is a most powerful thing to reflect on. Notice that the 'I' and the concept of trying to understand are both movements swimming in the undeniable sense of presence-awareness. From the deepest perspective, there is really no one there who needs to understand nor anything that needs to be understood. Awareness is. You are that. If you do a full stop right at that point, then—finished! Any remnant conceptualizing about this is just the old habits of the mind, which were geared toward looking for something 'out there' and in the future. But your own being is not out there nor is it in the future. It is not even 'in here' or in the present moment. Everything, including locations and times, takes place right in the fact of your clear, unobstructed being. Let the pointer resonate that there is absolutely nothing to get or understand which is not already present. Seeing this, the old concepts and beliefs get short-circuited.

Q: I can notice when I am getting caught up in the mental perspective and relax back into this. I know there really is not anything else I need to know because it is not about knowledge.

John: This is good. But now you are ready for the next step! Deeply inquire if there is really anyone there at all to get caught up or who needs to relax. Awareness is here in all its clarity. Just like the sky is never caught in the clouds, so is awareness never confined or limited by the appearances in the mind. You are that awareness. That is ever-free. Ultimately, you do not 'get' free. You understand or recognize your ever-present freedom. Continue to probe into this until it is completely clear.

Q: I feel like I am starting to fall into this more deeply. I have a sense that I am at least near the 'point of no return', if not past it, but at the same time, it is starting to seem like a practice and I know it should not be.

John: You do not fall into awareness more and more. You are awareness. Once you see that there is not a 'you' as one thing and awareness as something apart, the 'getting it and losing it' phase will drop away. Look and see if you are ever really apart from awareness. If you are not, then what do you have to do to become one with what you already are? Also the very sense of 'I', the notion of separation, is not really present. It is an assumption. If there is no separate 'I', then who is there to do or not do something? Looking at things along these lines will completely dismantle the conceptual framework from top to bottom. You will be left with the inescapable realization that what is—and always has been—is the natural state of already attained presence-awareness.

Q: I know that when I look inward, I cannot find anything substantial to hold onto and that thoughts are just ephemeral things in awareness like clouds in the sky. But I am still waiting for the 'I' to drop or at least become more transparent.

John: To really get to the root of these types of lingering questions and doubts, the most direct approach is to realize that every question and doubt hangs on the belief that the separate 'I' is present, that it is real and substantial. That is really the source of the apparent problem. The questions seem plausible, but they are actually based on a false premise. Expose that false premise and the doubts are severed at the root. That is the direct way to tackle this.

Q: I feel like there must be some substantial remaining blind spot I have that is keeping me in limbo.

John: Yes, the feeling that there is some separate 'I' in the picture, however nebulous. This is the last illusion. In truth, you are awareness now and always have been. Separation from that has never occurred, and thus all problems have absolutely no basis in any kind of fact.

Q: I will do all that I can do right now and just keep coming back to the basics as you have shown me. I cannot do anything else, but it just seems like it is harder than it should be, so I must be off-course somehow still.

John: The sense that something is hard or difficult implies a lingering belief that what is being pointed out has not yet occurred. But your own being is not an event. And is there any 'I' in the picture at all who needs to do or not do anything?

This all gets down to the recognition of something so clear and present that we tend to overlook it. Continue to come back to the basic points. They are so concise and simple that many times there is the tendency to run away to other issues and topics. But the answer always lies in what is simple, direct and certain. That which is most simple, most direct and most certain is that fact of being itself—your own being. In fact, it is utterly beyond doubt.

Q: After re-reading my comments a few times, I can see that these are all thoughts, too, and I can logically see the same advice you previously gave me applies here as well. I am just going to keep looking at this until it becomes completely clear to me. But I am sending this anyway because maintaining this dialogue has been very helpful for me. Thanks!

John: It is good to talk about this. The focus comes back again and again to the core points. Continue to look at all this for yourself and verify it in your own direct experience. When you see this for yourself, then you are beyond the need of pointers. They have done their job.

29

Knowing Blossoms Naturally

Question: Somehow, I know this is simple, and yet I am not able to get past the identification with the person. This reminds me of a situation a friend told me about. His daughter decided that she was actually a cat. She began acting like one and eating like one. She virtually lived like one. Then one day she told her father that she no longer wanted to be a cat, but she did not know how to stop being one and go back to being a person. Obviously there were some psychological issues, but he tried to explain to her that she was not a cat, that she did not need to do anything to become a person because that is what she already was.

It is funny how that absurd story would end up being so parallel to the most important understanding I could have. I am already awareness. I do not have to do anything to be that. Yet I still think I am a person. I do not know how to stop being one and just be what I am. I do not think a shrink can help me with this one.

John: Trying to stop being a person is just another modality of a person thinking he has something to do to get free. There is nothing to do or see or achieve, really. Just notice what the mind is doing. That is all! Whatever needs to happen, happens. Let anything come on the screen. All the ups and downs and gettings and losings are only dust devils spinning in empty space. There is no event, no moment, no wonderful mystic experience that confirms you or anyone is 'there'. That is the joke.

Understand that all pointers come back to a simple fact, the fact of being-awareness. It is not an event, an attainment, a moment of supreme wisdom that transforms a supposedly lost soul into the divine. An individual will never become a perfect, enlightened entity who has no problems, no demands, no activities. That is a pipe dream, just another passing dream before the unchanging gaze of awareness. Seeing your identity with awareness results in a natural abandoning of the concept of being a separate, individual entity. It is not about perfecting that concept!

Present awareness is divinity itself, perfection itself, love itself. It is here, it is you. If the thought comes up 'I do not get it', that thought is appearing right in the undeniable awareness. These pointers have struck home for you. The inner knowing blossoms naturally. You cannot force it or stop it. This knowledge which is resonating in your heart is far beyond being affected by the foibles of the mind or personality.

Let go of questions, doubts, worries, concerns and judgments. You do not need them anymore. Let your innate intelligence guide you. Live by courage and deep faith in life. Leave results to themselves. Take whatever you know or have resonated with and live by that to the best of your ability. Make your aspirations high and life will surely support you. Really give your heart and mind to pondering over the core pointers. The pointers are simple and few, but they need attention and application.

Disregard the doubts of the mind. Identify that in you which is present and aware. It is not difficult because it is always clear and available. You could have no thoughts, feelings or perceptions without your own conscious being. Take up headquarters there. Do that much, and everything will take care of itself.

30

The Central Character Is Utterly Non-Existent

Question: I have just finished reading the revised, second edition of *'Awaking to the Natural State'*. It is one of the clearest collections of writings on non-duality that I have come across. I am aware that the following is all mind stuff, but it has become a sticking point. In the manifestation, there is a body-mind that I normally think of as 'me'. I think of it as separate and existing in time and space.

John: In truth, it is just a series of appearances arising in awareness. Even the idea 'this is me' is just another thought. You stand as that ever-free awareness knowing it all. Your being, your nature as awareness, is never compromised or lost at all. There is just that idea arising. On deeper inspection the idea is seen as erroneous. Time and space are both concepts. Nothing ever exists separate from awareness. You can verify this for yourself through direct looking.

Q: From the perspective (for want of a better word) of presence-awareness, there is still a body-mind, but now it is not identified as 'me'. It is seen as an arising in awareness.

John: If you want to talk about 'from the perspective of present-awareness', then it is not really true to say that there is any separately existing object at all. It is all just a movement or appearance in awareness itself. It is made of awareness because it has no real existence apart from awareness. Do objects in a dream really exist? They appear to arise but have no substance or independent nature. They are really just the awareness or consciousness taking the form of a seeming object. The analogy of the waves and the water may be helpful to consider. From the perspective of presence-awareness itself, all there is is awareness or oneness. The sea is not concerned about the arising of waves, for nothing has ever really appeared with any independent substance apart from the water itself.

Q: Whether you are lost in the play or are aware that it is a play—in either case there is a kind of central character to the play.

John: The notion of a central character (and that character being my identity) is what I would bring under the most intense questioning and scrutiny. In the clearest teachings, the belief in a central character is completely dismantled. Other than a handful of thoughts, feelings and sensations passing in present awareness, is there anything you can point to with any substantiality or continuity at all, much less any central character?

If you think there is one, then try to find it. Other than a few momentary thoughts and sensations, what else is really there? There is not even a body, mind or world. These are all conceptual ideas but not actually given in direct experience. This may seem revolutionary but it is actual experience and easily verifiable. The mind creates conceptual realities that are not given in immediate experience and then lives by those mind-created concepts. The central one is the notion of being an autonomous and independently existing character. But, like I said, if it exists, you should be able to find it. I have never found one, have you?

Q: Then what is the nature of this body-mind? Why does it appear?

John: The question 'Why does the mind-body appear?' is concocted in the mind. It is important to notice that the mind is what has created or invented the notions of time, purpose and causality. After having formed these concepts, it tries to impose these categories on reality or 'what is'. But it is a futile endeavor. Like I always say, most questions are unsolvable at the level at which they are posed because they are based on unexamined premises that prove to be unfounded upon deeper inspection. It is a false question that is exposed as being absurd. In the seeing of that, the question drops. You do not solve a false question—you discard it. Or more precisely, when the false is seen as false, it drops away. It is just intelligence functioning.

Q: At one point in the book you say 'we are awareness experiencing through a body'. This seems to suggest that awareness is using the mind-body as a tool. Is this the case?

John: No! Awareness is beyond the mind and its categories. The notions of purpose, of tools and so on—not to mention all questions, doubts and problems—are generated at the level of conceptual thought. You cannot take these conceptual definitions and problems and impose them on awareness. Awareness is here. It is clear and doubtless. It has no problems, doubts or questions. It is really the light of life itself, the constant and immutable source of all appearances. It is also the source of peace or joy itself. Recognize that—and your identity with it—and all questions and problems are solved. At some point, it strikes home that the answers are simply not available to the mind. Period. Turn to the recognition of the clear and immediate presence-awareness that you are and you know everything that needs to be known.

Q: Still, I have to ask: what is the real nature of this central character that is undeniable but rarely acknowledged in spiritual teachings?

John: It is utterly non-existent. It is a fictional character that is imagined to be present but on investigation proves to be completely absent. See this for yourself and all questions, doubts and problems are annihilated completely at the root. You are left with the natural state of clear, open and undeniable being-awareness which is your true home and birthright. And there is not a problem or question in sight.

Q: Thank you for your illuminating reply. You are right, this does seem revolutionary! So, everything is an arising in awareness. Everything! The TV in the next room, this hand typing, this subtle thought of 'my hand typing'. Everything! It is completely airtight!

John: Yes!

Q: But this does leave the puzzle of why is there an imaginary central character in the first place? The imaginary character cannot be denied!

John: You keep saying so, but I keep denying it anyway! There is the appearance of a belief that a central character is present, but when looked for it, it is simply not there. Other than some thoughts assuming it is there, where is the thing in itself? This is a subtle point but proves to be true upon investigation.

Q: Although you say that all there is is just a handful of thoughts, feelings and sensations, these appear to form a recurrent theme in awareness. Ah, but wait a minute! Going on strictly present evidence I cannot say there is a 'recurrent theme' because that is just a thought arising presently. Right now there is no evidence of any appearances other than the present ones (except as a concept appearing presently!)

John: You are catching on!

Q: I suppose the 'why' in my question must be one of those big unanswerable questions that are usually answered with 'why not?' And, as you say, going in this direction is a futile endeavor.

John: It is not so much simply replying 'Why not?' There is more to it than that. You can see this more clearly by realizing that the question 'Why?' is based on certain factors, such as time, purpose, agency and causality. 'Why?' really means, 'What is the purpose?' It also implies there is some entity in the picture with a purpose in his or her mind. 'Why?' is really a meta-concept that depends on several other concepts. By concepts I mean mind-created categories that are not given in immediate experience. On deep and penetrating inquiry these concepts prove to be non-existent. They are provisional at best. 'Why?' turns out to be based on so many unverifiable and half-baked concepts that when this is seen the desire to even attempt to answer the question falls out of the picture. Like I say, you do not answer a false question, you discard it.

'Why does the character appear?' is one that is even easier to respond to. It is like saying why was the man-in-the-moon born? What can you say to that? Was he ever born? First find the character. If you find it, then we can talk about how it arose. Note that the concepts are clearly based on the assumption that it is there. But the question is, is it really there?

All the problems, doubts and seeking are for the character we imagine ourselves to be. But if it is found to be absent, what happens to all these things? They cannot continue, because the root it seen to be absent. Without a cause, can the effects remain?

You are zeroing in on the core issue. Keep in mind that throughout all of this discussion, present awareness remains clear, evident and beyond doubt. In the dismantling of the false concepts, your natural state of awareness shines out in all its clarity and obviousness. Concepts, thoughts and appearances never touch that in the least.

31

Talking About Spiritual Teachers

John: The tendency to talk about spiritual teachers, whether they are realized or not, which teaching is clearer and so on, is a complete diversion from the core understanding. It is a habit that simply diverts one away from the immediate and direct recognition of what is clear and available right in this moment.

There is no teacher outside and independent of us who 'has the understanding', has awakened, is enlightened or what have you. This kind of assumption leads to mistaken beliefs that just cloud the simplicity of what is being pointed to. There are a couple of problems with this way of thinking. First, the idea that teacher 'so-and-so' is realized has the implicit assumption for most of us that 'therefore, I am not'. Thus the belief in the sense of separation from our own presence is subtly strengthened. Second, talking about teachers who have it (or not) reinforces a belief that what is being pointed to is outside of ourselves—again emphasizing a sense of separation. Third, the teachers being discussed are usually not in our immediate environment and we are simply spinning in conceptual thought about people that are figments in imagination in that moment. Even if there were such a being as an enlightened teacher, if you approached them, the most you would find is a physical form composed of matter, chemicals and cells—which are just transient appearances in awareness. So the whole notion of beings who are awake or have the understanding is a complete fiction when looked at head on.

What is happening in this kind of thinking is that the attention is simply wandering in imagination and concepts. And the belief that reality is not present and that we exist as separate beings apart from it goes on without being exposed. Yet we can easily slip into statements such as, 'So-and-so is so clear', 'So-and-so has the understanding', 'Teacher X is realized, but teacher Y is not' and so on. Utter bullshit!

So what is this all about? What is being pointed to? It is the very fact of present awareness, which is completely clear and fully accessible right now. It is illuminating every thought, feeling and experience. That is the one and only reality to be understood or recognized. No teacher has this. It stands on its own, completely free of any particular people or their experiences. At best, a teacher is simply a sign post that can point back to what is real and present within you. There is no enlightened sign post. There is only the fact of being-awareness itself. As soon as we begin to talk about others who have it or not, we overlook the fact that it is fully present and shining as our own real nature here and now.

32

No Body, No Mind, No World

Question: I just read the following in one of your most recent articles:

'There is not even a body, mind or world. These are all conceptual ideas but not actually given in direct experience. This may seem revolutionary but it is actual experience and easily verifiable. The mind creates conceptual realities that are not given in immediate experience and then lives by those mind-created concepts'.

I do not recall ever hearing this stated like this and I am very intrigued. Could you please expand on this? How is this recognized in direct experience? Is it remnants in the belief in being a separate entity that is keeping this from being realized?

John: It is not really a mystical thing at all. For example, do you really ever experience a unified thing such as a body? On examination you only observe discrete sensations, feelings and perceptions. It is a constantly changing stream of events. For the sake of language we have created a label called 'body', but it is a makeshift verbal tool for the purpose of communication. It is the mind's attempt to organize a fluid and ever-changing series of states in order to talk about them. So 'body' is just a word, not a thing in itself. And yet we proceed to identify our being with a word when we say things like 'I am the body', 'When the body was born, I was born', 'When the body moves, I move', 'When the body is sick, I am sick', 'When the body dies, I die' and so on. You see how we live as if we are something that is really just a concept.

The same analysis goes for 'world', 'mind' and so on. We identify ourselves with conceptual ideas and live by them as if they were real. All suffering and confusion arises from this process. The truth is that here and now we are none of these things at all. We are the undeniable sense of being, which is present and brightly aware. It is illuminating all thoughts and concepts and never impacted in the slightest. It is not something to be known or realized because it is evident and clear right now. Can you deny your own being? Therefore, you stand fully self-realized now.

Everything else which arises is just a false idea. From this point, all we can do is dismantle, expose, challenge and question every concept that may arise. If you are looking for freedom, this will be the most exhilarating undertaking possible. If the tendency is to hold onto identities and beliefs, you are in for a rough ride because everything will get shot out from underneath you.

The Answer Is the Fact of Your Own Being

Question: I just read the section in your first book called *'Waiting for the Final Recognition'*. It goes straight to the point of it. I realize that it is the same basic points every time. But somehow the issue gets twisted around, and it seems like there is a new development and a new stall in the 'progress' that needs to be dealt with or lived through. But it is really just a failure to stay with the basics. This is always the issue.

John: The mind will try to throw up different concepts and puzzles that seem to be compelling. But they all boil down to a belief that somehow we are apart from the ever-present reality, and that we need to do something, get something or know something in order to be happy. The bottom line is that this is simply not true. The false ideas continue to be seen and exposed, and the clear and obvious truth of present awareness is recognized. Just keep in mind that you are not advancing toward or getting closer to anything that is not already the case. You just realize that the answer you have been seeking is the fact of your own being. It is effortlessly present and naturally attained.

There has never been a separate individual in need of something. It is just a simple fact that is pointed out. Innate intelligence recognizes it to be so. There is no problem in dismantling a few false ideas along the way if necessary.

34

This Moment of Pure Presence

Question: After we spoke, there was a bit of a letdown. I realize even that was whirling in this perfect presence. All of the accompanying emotions were seen and known as self-centered concepts. Like you say, there is nothing else to do but keep noticing. So even though there is this internal 'No!' when these concepts appear, they keep happening. They will keep coming up to be seen by no one.

John: Just remember it is not so much about getting rid of the stories or the conceptualization—because we do not choose or create them anyway. So how could we choose to get rid of them? We cannot. It is just a noticing of the ever-present perfection in each moment. Then the energy tends to drain out of the stories. Come right back to present awareness and the stories have no juice at all. In fact they are really hard to find. Ask yourself, 'In this moment, what and where are thoughts?' You immediately see how insubstantial they are. All our seeming problems are in thought. This is non-contestable. When you stop and look for thought in immediate experience it is really hard to pin down. Present awareness is much more clear, solid and well-known, even now. This is not a mystical understanding but just a direct knowing based on looking in present experience. All problems are just insubstantial threads of imagination hanging right in the clear and present being-awareness. As soon as you look at them, they dissolve.

You can also explore this in other ways. For example, is there even anyone present to whom the problems refer? And are not the ideas simply created in and made up of awareness anyway? So what is gained or lost? You never leave oneness even when conceptual thought seems to arise. From the highest level, there is nothing wrong at all. Nothing is really happening. No division in the oneness has ever occurred. There is no one present to do, see, understand or realize anything. There is just self-shining, ever-present awareness. The course is completely run right here and now. What is, is perfectly clear and obvious for each one of us. There is only this moment of pure presence. That is all there is.

35

What Is a Thought?

Question: I may be wording this poorly, but the question that still arises is, 'Why does the idea of a central character appear in the first place?' However, I am starting to realize that this sort of question is totally irrelevant. It is a bit like asking 'What is the meaning of life?' It is guaranteed to keep the mind spinning!

In your book, I love the way you continually stress that the mind cannot get this. Somewhere I know this for certain, yet I keep indulging in conceptual stuff. This must just be force of habit that will hopefully die down as these pointers take hold!

John: You are pushing back the boundaries of the question but you are running into the same problem. So you tell me— why does any thought arise at all? What is a thought? You will admit that any character (or belief in one) is completely an appearance in thought. And once thought is taken for granted, there can be endless objects, concepts, doubts and questions. For example, anything can happen in a dream once it starts because imagination is endless. So once there is thought, there is no reason why anything cannot be imagined. One of those imaginings is the belief in a central character. That happens to be the source of all suffering. From a practical perspective, the most important thing is to uncover the false belief and live free of suffering. That is why Buddha focused primarily on the cause and end of suffering and was not inclined to discuss speculative metaphysics and theories. If you want to be free of suffering, doubts and confusion just look at the basics and resolve the fundamental ignorance. There will be time later for philosophical niceties (if there remains any interest in such things!).

Anything that can appear at all is ultimately reducible to a thought or appearance in the mind. So the entire cosmos, both objectively and subjectively, can, for the sake of discussion, be represented by a single thought. Even the sense of 'I' is a thought. So a thought arises. Where did it come from? Why did it arise? How does it exist? Of what is it made? What is my relationship to that thought? A penetrating investigation of these questions will quickly lead you to a realization of your real identity and the true nature of appearances as well. Investigate this a bit and see what you come up with.

Q: Thank you for cutting through the fog. The funny thing is that deep down I know that the mind cannot get this. Right now all there is, is this. It is so obvious.

Just one small question, though. When you said 'anything that can appear at all is ultimately reducible to a thought or appearance in the mind' didn't you mean to say awareness rather than mind? Because to say all that can exist is an appearance in mind presupposes the existence of a mind!

John: Everything objective reduces to thought. But what does thought reduce to? That is what I am pointing you to. Is there any such thing as a thought apart from awareness? Thought arises and sets in awareness and is made of awareness. Recall the analogy of the water and the waves. Thought has no substance or reality whatsoever except as the awareness itself. All there is is awareness. What more is there? Non-duality means not-two, no separation. Everything, everywhere and at all times is that. You are that. Marinate in that a bit!

36

Ego, Awareness and I

Question: Since talking to you (and reading your material, along with books by 'Sailor' Bob and others) awareness has been 'arising' much more often.

John: Totally false. Awareness is the constant and unchanging background (and foreground, too!). It never rises or sets. If you succumb to this type of thinking then you are chasing your tail. You will be imagining that awareness comes and goes, that you do not have it and so on. The problem with reading about this is that the mind turns it into something other than what is being pointed to. This is not a mental understanding. In fact, there is nothing to be understood. It is a simple noticing of something so evident that we have overlooked it. If this is not precisely clear, the mind takes the words and tries to do something with them and wonders 'Where is the understanding?' Then you try to apply the pointers as some kind of exercise and things get very slippery.

Q: On the whole, I am more aware, more often, of what I am feeling and thinking.

John: This has nothing to do with what I am pointing to. Forget about the content and look directly into your present awareness.

Q: But nothing has 'clicked' and nothing 'stays' for any length of time.

John: That is because you are looking precisely 180 degrees away from the point! Time and states of experience are appearing and disappearing right in the ever clear and obvious presence that you are. There is nothing that needs to click or stay. These ideas are being generated by a misunderstanding of what is being communicated. Just see this and you can step out of this experience right now.

Q: I can always ask myself the questions such as 'Am I aware right now?' and so on. Immediately, I come back into an awareness of the 'open field' in which everything arises and falls away. But it feels like a trick or technique.

John: It is just a coming back and noticing something that happens to be so clear and obvious that we take it for granted. There is no more to it than this. The discovery of your real being leads to the recognition that everything we have been searching for is available right in the depths of the present moment. However, whether you notice it or not makes no difference to your true nature.

Q: But there is nothing about this that is self-sustaining or has changed my experience of life.

John: Who says that it is suppose to at all? That is another concept! However, as you sit with this and the fact of what awareness truly is sinks in, you will discover that all the doubts, questions, personal problems, searching for happiness and so forth are completely resolved. As I see it, that is a pretty worthwhile experience.

But at this point, you are taking this at an intellectual level. There is still a feeling that you are apart from awareness. As a seemingly separate entity you are looking for some benefit. Basically, the sense of identity and separation is not being questioned, and all the pointers are being looked at as if they are some kind of technique to apply so that the person will get a positive result. This is a common misunderstanding. It needs to be seen and discarded before any of this really starts to make sense.

Q: What seems to have happened is that there has been a split …

John: Right now is your being split? Is awareness split? Are you split? Are there two of you?

Q: Let me explain! Instead of being totally wrapped up in thoughts and emotions and for the most part 'unconscious', there are now two parts of my psyche. I admit that this is subjective and only how I am experiencing it. One part can be called the 'ego' (for lack of a better term). It is running a commentary and judging things and putting them into categories like good and bad. Then there is the second part, which is what I am calling awareness. It quietly and peacefully watches the other part.

John: You are turning awareness into some kind of mental construction. What you are calling 'awareness' is just another idea really. Then you have two ideas bouncing off of each other and creating duality. There is something even deeper that is present and untouched by all of this.

Q: For me, the ego keeps suffering and the awareness watches the suffering.

John: This proves that what you call awareness is really just another idea. Abiding in the actual awareness, the ego notion drops completely. The ego is the belief that you exist as a separate entity apart from your real being. The fact that this is confusing just shows that you are taking this at a mental level. Basically, you are thinking about it too much! The bottom line is that the identity of 'I am so and so' is still in play and not really being seriously examined.

Q: But both parts feel equally real.

John: Yes, because they are both just thoughts! If you believe thoughts to be real, then both sides of the thought-created equation are the same. It is just thoughts spinning and whirling and bouncing off of each other.

Q: The suffering continues ….

John: Because the real source of suffering is not being seen or inquired into at all. You need to ask yourself some deeper questions, such as—What is suffering? How does it arise? What is it based on? You cannot just pick up a few non-dual ideas and turn them over in the mind and expect some amazing result to follow!

Q: Not only is there the suffering of the original ego chatter and beliefs, but now there is what seems to be the suffering of the conflict between the two parts!

John: The person is left intact with all of his suffering. Then non-dual philosophy is added to the person as another belief structure or identity. It just becomes another link in the chain of bondage. Spiritual seekers, even those familiar with non-dual philosophy, are often wrapped up in immense suffering. The core of suffering is not really understood. Non-dual words have become just another adornment of the person who imagines he is limited and separate from the real.

Q: Awareness of course does not offer any resistance to anything, so it is not creating conflict. But 'I' (so I guess there must be three parts active at any given time!) feel conflict in trying to 'stay with' the awareness and not 'fall for' the ego part. It is a kind of cognitive/philosophical nightmare!

John: You are stumbling onto the root problem. The belief in the separate 'I' is the core driver of all questions, doubts and problems. The 'I' is still assumed to be in the picture and you are dancing in agony to the tune of its imagined problems. You need to question the idea that there is any such thing as an 'I' that is separate from awareness or even exists at all. As long as this is not questioned, you will continue to believe that 'you' are not there, that there is something wrong, that something needs to happen in order to be free and at peace. Taking the separation to be true and then attempting to get to awareness is futile. All the thoughts, strategies, techniques and tricks to heal the split are bound to fail.

You say 'I' and then proceed to talk about all the problems, doubts and stories of that 'I'. Yet from that position nothing seems to fit or feel right. Even trying to understand spiritual pointers based on non-duality just becomes a rat-hole that leads nowhere. But now you have seen that that is a dead end. The key lies in simply seeing and understanding what is going on. That is enough. There is nothing to do or fix, but the false can be seen to be false. And then the confusion drops away.

What is the 'I'? Get clear on that and all the doubts, problems and questions are undercut. As long as the 'I' is not investigated, then 'awareness', 'peace' and the rest are just empty concepts. What they are pointing to seems remote and unknown. Clear up the issue of your actual identity and you will discover that what is being pointed to is present in direct, nonconceptual knowing.

37

Leave the Mind to Itself

Question: I recently had an insight that there was no separate 'I'. For a couple of days after the insight, I did not pay much attention to thoughts. It was so obvious that they had nothing to offer. But unfortunately I find myself sliding back into the old self, and all of the old questions and dilemmas seem very important again.

John: When the sense of 'I' surfaces, problems start. Just see that. There is nothing else to do, just see it. If it is seen clearly that is enough.

Q: I know intellectually that I can never leave that which I am, nor can it fade. But I cannot help missing that which was such a peaceful and natural viewpoint (for lack of a better word).

John: Just notice that the mind creates the story in thought, based on the separate 'I', and the mirage of separation arises. Being-awareness is not really touched. After all, it is there knowing and lighting up the thoughts, isn't it? Just see this. It is enough to snap you out of it and bring you back to your true position (which you have never left!). Do not worry about thoughts appearing. There is no need to change anything (not that you can do so anyway!). Just turn to what is already present, clear and free. Leave the mind to itself.

Q: I do not feel I can 'get back' with my own will-power.

John: Which 'I' are you talking about? If you think one is there, find it and show it to me!

Q: I realize that this originates from the belief that there is someone here, and I saw that night that there is no one! I did not do anything. It just happened when reading a book. I do not even feel that looking for the 'I' will do it. I have done that many times and it only gives me an intellectual answer. So, now, life is about 'me' again. The same worries and pain are back. I feel self-centered and limited. Is there anything I can do?

John: Which 'I', please? This is just more self-centered thinking based on the assumption of an 'I'. That is all. Just see what is happening. There is nothing you can do, because you—as a separate 'I'—are not there anyway.

Q: So any doing is from the 'me', until we see it isn't. I did see this—and that is why it is so weird that I cannot see it now!

John: Look for the 'I'. You will not be able to find it. Then where else are you but with the recognition of ever-present, 'I'-less awareness?

Q: Somewhere in your book you say that even wanting to be rid of suffering as a special undertaking is a trap. What did you mean there?

John: Who is trying to get rid of suffering? The apparent 'I'. So it is just an activity based on the false belief in a separate 'I' and leads nowhere.

Q: I hope to be done with all this soon!

John: Again, which 'I' are you talking about? You will be done when you are convinced that the 'I' has never been there at all. That is the case now. Just see it.

38

Clarity Is Its Own Confirmation

Question: Thank you very much for writing and putting me back on course as far as where to look. I can see what you are saying about looking 180 degrees in the wrong direction. When I look in the right direction, not only is 'it' (just this) absolutely apparent, but all questions dissolve instantly. It is seen that any question that I could raise would just be the false sense of 'me' spinning out questions, thoughts and ideas as it has done all my life.

There are moments when new questions will arise and I will think, 'Oh, John makes a good point, but what about this or that?' But when I look and see, I can see that it is just more of the same thought story and that nothing is really obscured in any way. Then the questions fade again. It is amazingly subtle how ideas will creep into my awareness and, if not seen, are taken to be the truth. That is obviously what leads to the sense of having lost it.

What I keep missing when this happens is that no thoughts are true. Everything is just what is arising and falling away in awareness. When I get stuck, it is always because something like the following happens—'Well, I am aware that these six things are false, mind-generated stories, but this other one (whatever it might be) is true'. It helps to be reminded that the mind will never get this. It is also helpful for me to remind myself that it is all mind stuff. There is not some false mind stuff and some true mind stuff. So for now, there is nothing to ask! I can see the thought arise, 'I am going to lose it again and then I'll have to talk to John again'. But then it is seen through.

I cannot thank you enough, John, for your time and assistance. I hope you will never be hearing from me again! I hope that I never feel I have lost it again and need you to set me straight. But even that is just another story about the future. If it happens it will just be a part of what is in that moment. Thank you so much!

John: You are on a roll with this! What you are communicating is clear. You do not need my confirmation. Your insights are your own. Clarity is its own confirmation. Feel free to stay in touch as the spirit moves!

39

Everything You Need Is Right Within You

Question: Just a quick note to again express my gratitude. A few days ago (after our week of dialogue), I set out for a long walk along the Cornish coastline. After about four miles I sat down for a rest and stared out at the sea. At once there was a total recognition that time does not—cannot—exist! It was a non-mental, direct recognition that there is no past or future. There is just this unfolding, living edge, moment by moment, always utterly fresh. With this recognition, the question of separation was meaningless. It is as if there could be no room for separation. There is just this one big unfolding, which contains everything! With this came a tremendous sense of relief and the certainty that this is the real state of things!

Now the important thing here is that I have had this taste before. And almost immediately the mind comes in and tries to make sense of it, which eventually leads to a 'yes, but ...' moment. On this occasion that did not happen. The mind did try to spin out, but there was a spontaneous and completely effortless sense that it was pointless and irrelevant to go there. Your total and uncompromising insistence that the mind cannot get this seems to be taking hold!

Of course, a few days later as I get on with my life, job, family, business and so on, I am back in a kind of semi-diverted mode. But now there is a sense of certitude that this really cannot be lost. With this is a bubbling sense of well being! So, again, thank you, John!

John: I enjoyed reading your insights. You can be sure the recognition of your true nature is clear for you. You do not need me to confirm this. Our dialogues have exposed the mind and all of its conceptual underpinnings. Everything you need is right within you as the undeniable fact of ever-present, ever-clear awareness. You have seen that separation is false. It is nothing more than a concept. Now you have seen and experienced that the cause of the individual, personal life lived in separation is not true.

This understanding will continue to reveal itself spontaneously and naturally. It is like emerging from a fog bank into bright sunlight. Now you know that light to be the light of your own real being. What you discover is that in truth the sunlight was never in the fog bank at all. It is what is knowing the fog bank and all else. It has been utterly free from the start. At this point, there is not much more I can say. But feel free to stay in touch as the spirit moves.

40

Taking Things Personally Goes

Question: I love reading the articles on your website and feel a lot of resonance. But surely when this 'I' is seen through, not all problems and conflicts just disappear!? There is still a life being lived, which on a day-to-day basis can be very challenging. For example, if my husband suddenly decides to go to the pub every night and leave me to look after our baby, that is going to cause conflict if I am not happy with that. Also, if my husband starts spending all our household money without asking me, this would also cause conflict. So, even if the 'I' is seen for what it is, surely there is still going to be many problems to sort out. I would so much appreciate your view on this. Kind regards.

John: Life goes on. There are events, decisions and things to work out. The whole universe is a vast sea of activity, after all. However, the sense of having personal problems disappears. There is just the mind and body functioning in the light of intelligence. Things go a certain way or not, but the concern over the outcome is gone. There can be tremendous care and intelligence applied. All the thoughts and feelings go on just fine. But taking things personally goes.

So, personal suffering, doubt, confusion anxiety and so forth are left behind. The reason is that the separate person who previously owned or identified with things is removed from the picture. It has nothing to do with the outer events or situations. Do you get what I am pointing to?

Q: I think I get what you are pointing to. Problems, thoughts, feelings and so on continue to arise. But when the

'I' is seen through then there is no one to take hold of them and identify with them. So situations still arise and are dealt with but without the tension and identifying as a separate individual doer. Am I understanding this correctly?

John: Bingo! Perfect!

Q: I hope you do not mind me asking another question. However, I do understand that the questions that the 'me' asks are a bottomless pit!

John: Your intuition is true! Questions are an expression of a fundamental sense of doubt or unease about ourselves. The mind, in sensing this fundamental uneasiness, is pressed into service to work things out, but it comes up short until the basic issues are exposed.

Q: At this moment, though, some questions are still arising for me.

John: Ultimately, you will need to get back to the basic issue of resolving your identity. Until then, the questions and doubts go on. Sometimes they shift to other levels and topics, just like the manifestations of a disease can erupt elsewhere if the symptoms are suppressed.

Q: If, for instance, you are an alcoholic or drug addict, then I am presuming that actions are still taken to find a cure, such as therapy, hypnotherapy, counseling and so forth.

John: That could arise as part of an intelligent response. It likely will not cure the fundamental metaphysical issues, but could at least provide some relative support to the body and mind.

Q: Also, if someone's character is very jealous and insecure then there could be steps taken to heal this.

John: I suppose there are some relative steps that could be taken through counseling or whatever to begin to address these types of things at a certain level. Why not? This is not in conflict with a deeper investigation into the roots of things. Like I said, though, these relative approaches may have an effect at a certain level, but are not likely to get to the roots of the fundamental questions, such as 'What is my true nature?' and 'What is the ultimate source of suffering?' This does not necessarily imply that we throw overboard all such relative approaches as useless. They have a use at the level at which they apply.

In general, the ultimate source of suffering is not usually fully addressed by the standard types of counseling and therapy. They may be good but might not have the full answers. That needs to be tested and verified in one's own experience.

Q: Am I seeing all this correctly?

John: You need to look for yourself and test your findings against your own experience, intuition and judgment. Do not downplay your own judgment in all this. I am just pointing to something which has made a difference for me, but you need to find answers that are true for you and fit your experience.

41

You Are the Reality Itself

Question: I guess I am still expecting fireworks. I remember last year sitting outside my flat at three in the morning sharing a few glasses of wine with a friend, saying that the thing I wanted most in life was to experience enlightenment!

This was before the teachings of non-duality found me and things became clearer. But the desire for an experience remains a sticking point to some extent. While I know that what this is about is *'The Simple Feeling of Being'* (to quote the title of an excellent book by Ken Wilber), that brightly alive feeling of presence, a part of me is still expecting something different, something special, a shift in perception of some kind.

Maybe I have read too many stories by people who have experienced awakening, enlightenment, kensho, a loss of self or 'I', and a feeling of unity or oneness with everything. It seems these stories have created a set of concepts and expectations about what it must be like, which my mind still plays with. All I can do is be aware that they are just thoughts and concepts that have no reality and that the mind loves to play around with. How can it possibly be like anything the mind can conceive of?

There is still a groping towards understanding and clarity. There is still an idea that something will suddenly click and all will be as clear for me as it is for you. I sometimes wonder what the difference is between your understanding of this and mine and whether or not there is such a thing as a sudden shift in perception or recognition or understanding. Thanks once again for your good work.

John: Bob Adamson cured me of the concept of enlightenment. Basically, there is no such thing as getting enlightened as some future event. If you are sitting around waiting for something to happen, you are barking up the wrong tree. That would have nothing to do with what is being pointed to. In all truth, there is really no awakening or enlightenment at all. This is one of the last concepts that the mind hangs on to. So forget about that completely!

Being-awareness is here in all its fullness right now. That is it. That is what you are and always have been. Full stop. End of the road. Everything else that comes up is a false concept based on the belief in a separate individual that is apart from the real. You are not a limited person apart from reality. You are the reality itself.

As you sit with this and resonate with it, everything will spring from there without effort. The idea before was that you were not there. I assure you that you are there. So why are you waiting for some event or for something to click? If you feel you need to do something, then question, challenge and expose any concept that is contrary to this fundamental point.

42

All Problems Are False Problems

Question: We spoke briefly sometime last summer when I discovered 'Sailor' Bob Adamson's book. Since then I also ordered and have devoured most of your book, *'Awakening to the Natural State'*.

There is something so clear about what is being presented, but I feel I need a final push to fully clear up the lingering notions of separation and to be able to rely on that which you and Bob point to—pure awareness of the fact of our existence. Like you stated in your book, unless we clear up a few remaining doubts and lingering misunderstandings about our real identity and the falseness of the perceived 'I', we will remain on the hamster wheel indefinitely spinning our wheels trying to be what we already are.

Could you help me let go of what I am still holding onto and help me bridge the gap to the natural state of being? I am stuck and have gotten as far as possible reading it in books. I have often times even known that I know the ever-present awareness that never moves and is untouched by appearances. Yet the issue with the separate entity is still kicking my ass, though not nearly as painfully as it once use to.

I know you have been here and are probably reading this saying, 'It is just so simple!' I agree. So what I am asking is to hear it from the horse's mouth and to get that final push to clear up the fog that keeps it from appearing, even though it never goes or comes but just is. I suppose it sounds like I half-heartedly understand this.

John: I would be happy to talk with you about this.

Q: Thanks for the offer to discuss this. It is apparent that one or both of the two basic understandings are being just slightly missed. The first is that awareness is my true being/self/identity and that all else appears in presence upon that awareness.

John: This is pointed out. You need to look into this to verify that being-awareness is your real and unchanging nature. It is not so much a matter of thought, but of looking and verifying this in immediate experience.

Q: The second point is that there is no 'I' that needs to get anything (or to be dropped for that matter)!

John: Yes. Although we often refer to ourselves as a separate 'I' with various qualities and attributes (such as not being enlightened yet!), we do not recognize that there is really no such being in the picture at all. Enlightenment or non-enlightenment are just attributes or states of a being who imagines itself to be present and apart from the reality. That is why all the problems, questions and doubts are moot until the issue of the 'I' is resolved. If the 'I' is false, then everything else turns out to be a false problem. You do not solve a false problem, you see it as false. In the seeing, it drops away—along with all the dilemmas hanging on it.

Q: Is it that simple?

John: Yes.

Q: And who would be the one to inquire who is asking 'Who am I?'?

John: Who is asking?

Q: You once said I am looking in the wrong direction. So in what direction should the looking take place?

John: The wrong direction is looking into concepts based on false premises. The heart of the problem is then overlooked. So come back to the real issues, which are the discovery of your real identity and the seeing through of the false one. I would call that a more productive direction to inquire.

Q: All of this resonates very clearly. The pieces of the puzzle are coming together. I do not know what else to say or ask.

John: Stay right there and notice that you are precisely right where you need to be. Everything you are looking for is present. The fact of being is clear. The fact of awareness is here. You are that and can never be anything other than that. In this sense, the course is run. In the spiritual search, the most important thing is what you are seeing right now. If the mind kicks up a contrary idea, just see it for what it is—an idea arising in present awareness. Everything else is a concept, but you—as presence-awareness—are not a concept. You are that light illuminating concepts and all else. Under no circumstances can you ever leave what you are. There is nothing you need to do, get or know to be present and aware. It is your natural birth right. Sit with this and let everything unfold from this knowing.

There is No 'Who' or 'Why'

Question: I have been sitting with it as you suggested back in January and also re-reading our exchange. One of the things you said then helped nudge my understanding. I am writing again in the hope that you will provide another pearl in response to this new question that has arisen!

You said: 'The whole thing about awareness and content is a little artificial . . . So there is no content, only awareness'. I now see that that is true. I was in danger of thinking that there was awareness and something separate that awareness is aware of. But now I see that it is all one stuff, just being what is. I am also clear that there is no real 'me' or 'I' either. At most, all that can be found are passing thoughts which tend to have a common theme that relates to things that happen to and around this body labeled 'Tom' or sometimes 'Daddy' (or sometimes worse names!). But these thoughts all relate to a non-existent entity, because there is simply nothing here.

So if there is no separate entity, then I am everything that appears. I am the experiencing of that. But I am not a thing. I am no-thing. And nothing needs to be done for that to be the case. It always just is, just happening as it is.

This being the case, I am left wondering who is in fact having all these dialogues and questions of the type on your website or in your book and why? If there is no 'me' here and no 'you' there, then who is talking to whom and why is this happening? Indeed, in many of your responses you refer to a 'you', such as 'You are getting the hang of this!' or 'You are going to see some profound shifts'. But surely there is no 'you' there for whom this is true, but the remarks are being addressed to someone or something and the exchanges are happening?

So it seems to me that each exchange, each question, each thought is simply arising by itself as part of the appearance in response to other conditionings or reasons and they just bounce back and forth but really have no real purpose because they speak of things that do not exist. The exchanges appear to deal with non-existent apparent questioners (like me!) who think they need questions answered. But that it is in fact all just part of the show with no actors!

So who is talking to whom and why?

John: The questions go on until the questioner realizes that his imagined existence as a separate entity is a complete fiction. Then the questioner is disposed of along with the questions. Trying to find the one who is asking and answering is still continuing to look in the mind for an answer. Of course all the questions and answers are based on false assumptions and are not ultimately valid. The assumed seeker brings up questions. Answers are given to dismantle the questions and—more importantly—the questioner himself.

All words and teachings are only relative. They are makeshift and temporary and have no intrinsic value in themselves. Even your current questions are just empty mind stuff. The mind wants clarity and answers. It imagines separation and creates suffering and doubts. It raises questions and looks for answers. There is no answer to 'who' and 'why' because there is no 'who' and no 'why'. These are just imagined concepts that fall to pieces when scrutinized. Who is it that is asking questions? And why is there a question at all when you are the ultimate reality itself?

In the end, the answer is simply the fact of your own being, that undeniable presence of awareness shining at your core. It is pointed out and the oneness that was never lost is apparently recovered. So let go of the mind and be what you always have been—the ever-present obvious fact of being-awareness. There is nothing which exists with any independent nature apart from this. This awareness, your real being, is all there is. Now you know everything I can possibly tell you. What I am is not different from what you are. There is only that.

44

The Crucial Question

John: In present experience there is the undeniable fact of your conscious being. Make sure this is clear. Everything else that appears must be a thought, a feeling or a bodily sensation. These are appearing in the ever-present and clear awareness that you are. Those appearances never touch or modify being-awareness. Make sure to understand this. Other than the above items, there is nothing else in our field of experience. There is just awareness and some thoughts, feelings or sensations passing through.

All problems, doubts and questions (collectively called 'suffering') are just thoughts. Verify this for yourself. All suffering is for someone, for a person who imagines himself or herself to be limited and separate. Thus, all suffering and doubts are really just self-centered thinking. Self-centered thoughts are simply thoughts that revolve around the assumption of the existence of a separate self. So the idea of a separate 'I' is the foundation upon which all self-centered thinking is based. Self-centered thinking always presumes that the 'I' is present and real and that this is what we are.

But is this really true? Are we a limited 'I' or are we the fact of being-awareness? This is the crucial question. If there is any such thing as a limited 'I' or separate self, you should be able to find it. Is there any thought, feeling or sensation that I am prepared to call myself? No, since those are all temporary appearances. Then what else is there that I can find that could be this presumed separate 'I'? Can you find anything else at all?

If the 'I' cannot be found, then who has a problem, who is not good enough, who needs to attain something and so forth? Yet the fact of your being, as present awareness, is perfectly clear and obvious. The nature of being-awareness is also clarity or peace. As this is known more clearly, a life in clarity is realized as the natural state.

There are two main points here. The first is that your actual nature or being is recognized to be awareness or consciousness. The second is that suffering is investigated and its cause is discovered to be absent. This investigation has the result of removing the root cause of suffering, which is the imagined sense of separation from our real source. And without the cause can the effects remain? Seeing all this is neither a difficult nor a protracted process. It is really just seeing the actual state of affairs. What remains is the ever-present natural state.

Look at this for yourself and verify it in your own experience. Do not take my word for it, but investigate it to your own satisfaction.

45

The Doubtless Sense of Existence-Awareness

Question: I was thinking today about how absolutely everything refers to 'me' and 'my' relationship to 'it'. It is all about how 'I' can best survive in competition with every other being. It is the same personal story for everyone. I can see that a life of seeking is a strategy to achieve security or escape the fear associated with being 'me'. There is nothing new here. It is just the human story doing its thing. You and others have pointed out that the belief in a separate 'I' is the root cause of our problems. For example, you say, 'You need to question the idea that there is any such thing as 'I' that is separate from awareness, or even exists at all. As long as this is not questioned, you will continue to believe that 'you' are not there, that there is something wrong, that something needs to happen in order to be free and at peace'.

I always find this inquiry a slippery thing to do. Frankly, I feel stuck. Because I can see myself looking for a technique, such as 'Who am I?' or 'Who is asking?' and so on. I do not truly understand what is going on, and the confusion is mounting. I admit I am thinking too much! But tell me this, if there is no 'I' that is thinking too much or even assuming the notion of a separate identity, then what moves this predicament on from this intellectual impasse?

John: Basically, it involves a clear seeing of the facts as they are. As I always say, everything of a problematic nature (suffering, doubts, questions, personal issues and so on) is for the separate sense of 'I'. This can also be stated as all problems are for the imagined person. It all gets down to what we take to be the 'I'. That not being clear, all kinds of ideas, troubles and identities are associated with who we think we are. But it is all confusing and lacks any reality because we are not clear on what our true nature is.

I would suggest putting all other questions and problems on hold temporarily because they cannot be adequately resolved until the matter of the 'I' is addressed thoroughly. This is not a matter of thinking it out and unraveling the mental questions. Think too much and you lose the simplicity of this. If that is going to be the approach, then is it better to just go out and have some fun and forget about spirituality completely. You will be much happier. I mean this in all sincerity.

If you still want to get into all this, I would next recommend that you tackle things from the positive side first. The most important realization is to see what is being pointed to as your true nature. There is in you now—not as a speculation—a sense of presence or existence. Whatever it is, it is also aware. So there is that undeniable sense of existence-awareness in you right now. It is present and registering everything. This cannot be grasped through words because it has nothing to do with words. It is so simple and evident that we overlook it. The mind can do nothing with this because the mind appears in what is being pointed to.

Anyway, this presence, for lack of a better word, is what is being pointed to. Can you deny the fact of your being or your awareness? Begin to recognize that this is the space in which everything (thoughts, feelings and perceptions) arises. This needs to be clear and there needs to be some resonance with this before you can productively look at anything else. If this is not clear everything becomes mental speculation. So start by exploring this doubtless sense of existence-awareness with you right now. Get back to me and see what you come up with.

121

46

There Is No Seeker Left to Tell His Story

Question: Your posts have burned through a lot of the crap. I am grateful. Still the pendulum swings wildly. I am dealing with recurring thoughts such as 'I love myself, I hate myself. I love you, I hate you'. What now?

John: The pendulum swings back and forth. That is its nature. For some period of time we are focused on the pendulum and its movements. This pendulum is the sense of 'I' that we have been conditioned to view as our self. Then the attention gets directed from the pendulum to the space in which it appears. The space never swings or moves. It is steady, clear and un-affected by all movements. It is an empty, clear, content-less container. Without it, there could be no pendulum, no move-ment, and nothing to focus on. No matter how much the pen-dulum swings, it cannot reach the space or become the space. It cannot even know the space.

No amount of seeking, asserting or willing can achieve this recognition. It is a wordless, imageless, and non-conceptual re-alization that often arises when one has developed a sense of communion and rapport with one who has realized this. The recognition arises as a spontaneous and unexpected knowing that is utterly beyond the ability to manufacture or attain from the position of a separate person. It is completely fresh and new, yet deeply familiar. It is a stirring of the innate awareness itself in response to a very clear pointing. Ultimately, it is the simple recognition of the presence of awareness that is clear and beyond doubt, even now. That is the simple truth of it.

The focus on the story of the individual acts as static that obscures the initial stirrings of the resonance. As the false beliefs and stories are exposed and dismantled, the resonance breaks forth with more and more clarity. The resonance is more subtle than the usual thoughts and feelings of the embodied person which we have lived with as our habitual identity. We are apt to overlook the living understanding as long as the focus is on the grosser manifestations of the person. Still, there is some recognition. It may take some time for it to blossom into a steady and clear lived experience, but with the right spirit of inquiry and uncompromising guidance, all obstacles can be overcome. The one who was seeking and suffering recovers his natural condition, not as an asserted achievement but as an actual living cognition of the fact of presence-awareness. There is nothing one can do to achieve this because the one attempting to get the experience is the static itself.

Through trust and deep faith in what is being communicated, the apparent seeker will be completely dissolved as a separate entity. In that dissolution, the dawn of clear wisdom breaks forth. No words need be communicated about it. It is a clear conviction that the seeking is over, what needs to be known is known. There is no seeker left to tell his story because he has been totally dissolved and no one remains who one could meaningfully talk about. Whatever words come forth will have no reference to a person or his stories, his attainments or ups and downs. The paradox is that there is no one left who can claim it or talk about it. So the autobiography can never be completed. The protagonist has left the premises. All there is is empty space and clear awareness in all directions. From that, there may arise a communication—or not. It is just a sharing of, or pointing to, the simple fact of being. And that is what you are now.

47

Who You Are Is Not Bland or Mediocre

Question: In my first e-mails to you of some six months back, I complained that although there was a clear and definite recognition of 'my' absence, it did not seem to be accompanied by bliss. I did not care about having a mind-blowing experience, but I did care to be just plain happier, and my average level of happiness did not seem to be appreciably improved.

Now, although still not experiencing much elation, not much exuberance for life, but rather usually just feeling mediocre and even still grumpy at times, it is no longer of much concern. Perhaps there is more happiness than before, perhaps not. But the seeking for happiness seems to have dropped away and I appear to be content with that mediocrity. There is still an interest in happiness, but not a struggle for it. And so there is more peace now, and I think that more peace is a precursor (not a cause) of more happiness. But even if it does not show up, having lost my concern for happiness, I am definitely feeling better! So, I am happy about that!

John: At some point, the checking in for the separate self falls away because you have just verified that it is not there. Once seen, no ongoing checking is needed. Actually, the pointer to rest as the natural awareness is still a half-step. Who is being asked to rest? Is there anyone who is not that natural awareness? I am sure you see all this, but I am just underscoring that even the need to check for the self and/or rest as awareness is still very subtly associated with thought, so that can fall away.

Elation is just a state. Anything that can come, will go. Awareness is inherently free, open, peaceful, steady. That does not need to be brought in. The false concepts drop away and the ever-present state of presence-awareness is seen for what it is. Then, the feeling is more like 'there is nothing wrong anymore', as Nisargadatta Maharaj said. But you are not looking for states of the body and mind to be a certain way.

The feeling of being mediocre is not given in non-conceptual, immediate experience. It feels more like an evaluation by the mind, with perhaps a residual bit of judgment. 'I appear to be content with that mediocrity'. Maybe that is just a way of saying that you realize that you are the ever-fresh, bright and sparkling awareness that shines like a million suns and within which the universe rises and sets. From that position, everything that arises is fine just as is. Words can be deceiving!

Q: This is spot-on, John. Right on target and so well put. Thank you. What you wrote about the need to check in and your take on mediocre experiences is very excellent.

John: Remember, who you are is not bland or mediocre! You are the principle of life, light and love that makes all experience possible.

48

Love Is Always in the Present

Question: Your writing has been a revelation for me. Thank you. I have a question. Does awareness have an arrow of attention or focus?

John: Not really. Awareness is wide open and omni-directional. It is registering everything. Ultimately, it is beyond form, parts, time and space. All these things appear within it. Things like focus, attention and direction apply to the mind or the senses, that is, the instruments within awareness. The mind may focus or not, but awareness is taking it all in. Whether the mind is focused or not, everything is registered by that knowing principle within you.

Q: Does awareness get directed back towards itself, so that there is awareness of awareness only?

John: No! Awareness is never an object. You cannot split it into parts, with one being turned back on itself. Sometimes the mind in its attempts to grapple with this falls into these conundrums. The truth is that it is much simpler than all that. Awareness is here now. It is clear, open, doubtless and shining right within you. You can say that it is self-knowing. Awareness knows itself immediately and without subject/object duality. It is just the simple fact of present awareness that is here beyond all doubt.

Q: I have a basic understanding that awareness is all that there is. Still thoughts seem to command a lot of attention.

John: As long as there is a subtle belief in the reality of thoughts or a sense, however vague, that what we are is some kind of entity or person in the appearance, the fascination with thoughts goes on. Just note that whether thoughts appear or not, awareness shines free and clear and is never obscured. It is just the natural condition. Awareness has no need to do anything with thoughts. Both thoughts and attention to thoughts are coming in at the mind level. Awareness stands beyond, naturally free.

~ Follow up ~

Q: I faced where you pointed and what came to me was the invitation to abandon thought and live in love. I am happy. The seeking seems to be done. Thank you for all this.

John: Nice to hear from you. 'Abandon thought and live in love'. Nicely put. The direct, non-conceptual, non-mental recognition of open awareness or being is love. So when we talk about awareness, this is also love. In relation to thought, our real being appears as the awareness illuminating thought. In relation to feelings, it is the light of love in which feelings arise and set. In itself, it is one wordless presence—the natural state.

Keep in mind that once you recognize this, thought and activity go on quite well. It is not so much an abandonment of thought as a release of attachment or sense of identity with the story of a separate 'me' woven in thought. Till now that has been our reality, but once life in love and open awareness is recognized, the attachment or belief in the reality of the conceptual story of 'me' is dissolved. Love is a solvent that dissolves all concepts of self, separation, time, space and all categories woven by the conceptual mind. Love is always in the present and completely outside of the web of thought. It is ever-present and shining as your unchanging core, the simple fact of luminous being. Another word for it is the heart, which means your true center. I am glad to hear this recognition is clear. That is what this is all about.

49

Non-Duality, Suffering and What Is

Question: In your book, you say that there are non-dualists who say that suffering, war, killing, evil and so on are part of the divine or part of what is. You say that you do not really go in for that approach. Well, I guess I am one of those who see the 'evil' part of life as just an expression of awareness! It would be nice to say that the divine is all good and loving and that 'evil' and 'suffering' are just wrong thinking and ignorance that we can overcome by clear seeing, but this is just what Christianity and other religions are saying. A few word changes for non-dualism and we have separation, sin, the Fall and salvation. But who is it that is separate? And who is it that is in ignorance? And who is it that investigates? And who is it that sees? As non-dualism says, there is no person there, so why does non-dualism blame the mind, thought and ignorance for the separation when these are also just expressions of what is? Who is there to make the choice and who is there to be responsible? Non-dualism's answer to this is no one is there. So how can anything, even the evil and killing and separation, be anything other than awareness expressing itself in life?

So the seeker, the thinker, the believer, the questioner, the person living in his mind and the person dominated by ego are all the actions of awareness and there is nothing wrong with it. Even one who sees reality as it is can still question, read, think and be in the mind if that is how awareness chooses to continue the role of that expression. It makes no difference. There is no one there other than the characters that awareness is expressing. That is all there is.

I find non-dualism falling just as short as all the other

teachings. In the end, all we can say—if awareness so moves us to do so—is that all there is, is all that is. Hopefully, we can rest and live in that certainty and peace, living life to its fullness as awareness so expresses itself in each of us. In coming to see this, there is a knowing and confidence and peace there. I have come to live in an awareness of that presence. Nothing else matters any more.

John: Your understanding is very clear. I have no quarrel with it. My sense is that there is very little that I can point to that you do not already know. However, the following is coming up in response to your comments.

All words, teachings and pointers fall short. This you have seen. To try to get a clear and accurate expression is a futile effort. All that matters, if anything matters, is the direct non-conceptual recognition of present awareness and our identity with that. Even that does not really matter because whether there is a recognition or not, we are still only that. All teachings—even your own attempts to express how non-duality falls short—are provisional. There is no accurate pointer or word, none at all. You express your vision very clearly, but then, like all of us do, you lapse into hopeless contradiction, as in the following:

'... hopefully we can rest and live in that certainty and peace, living life to its fullness as awareness so expresses itself in each of us. In coming to see this, there is a knowing and confidence and peace there. I have come to live in an awareness of that presence. Nothing else matters any more'.

Who is hopeful? Who is the 'we' that can hopefully rest and live in certainty? Who needs to live life to its fullest? Who has come to live in awareness? When all there is is that and there is no separation from that, there is no one there who needs to hope, rest, live and so on. I know that you realize this

130

and have expressed the same. I am just pointing out the fact that all language and expression is appearing in dualism and tends, by its nature, to create false divisions. Once that is seen, you can use language, being fully aware of its limits.

Non-duality means no separation, nothing other than the one. Any appearance, thought or experience is only that. So there is really nothing to say or to express at all. It is like standing on the North Pole. Whichever way you move, you start heading south again. So once you start to say anything, you immediately suggest false dualisms. Even the teaching of non-duality is false. Like all paths, it is just a pointer. All pointers are false because there is only oneness. There is no need for a path because you are already what you are seeking.

Realizing this, there is no need to say or do anything. However, if there is a communication in speech, actions or writings, those expressions will carry a fragrance of living understanding. The words, though false in themselves, will awaken a resonance. If the words are left behind and the inner resonance is followed, the understanding will arise in the apparent other of something utterly beyond words and thoughts. In words, this is hopelessly incomprehensible. But those who relinquish words in favor of immediate inner knowing realize a depth of peace and certitude that is the most real and intimate experience of life.

Yes, ultimately everything is only the oneness, including war, crime, murder, brutality, mayhem and so on. However, these acts and expressions generally arise out of a fundamental basic ignorance, the belief in the existence of a separate 'I' apart from the oneness. Rather than speak of these things as an expression of the one, which is strictly true, I am inclined to trace their source to its root cause. I am more interested in the living experience of clarity and the resolution of human suffering rather than maintaining an extreme non-dual stance in language. That is just my expression of the oneness!

There is a style of non-dual teachings that say that all our ignorance, suffering, separation is just the one, therefore just accept them as 'what is'. For some, this style resonates and works. However, I find that there is something too assertive and idealistic about it for my taste. The bottom line is that teachers in this vein still talk about people waking up, recognizing oneness, being lost in stories, oscillating between recognition and non-recognition, and all the rest. Plus they show up to teach apparent others and so forth. So the behavior actually contradicts the radical non-dualistic position expressed verbally. In some cases, the statement that 'all is one' is really just a mental assertion. Why tolerate separation and suffering when it can be directly resolved through clear seeing? If this is dualistic then so be it. It makes no difference to the oneness. Those who view their suffering, pain, separation and seeking as the divine are most welcome to keep them! For my part, I encountered a clear and decisive remedy for these things through the teachings and guidance given by Nisargadatta Maharaj and 'Sailor' Bob Adamson.

I prefer to be a bit more down to earth and practical, even at the risk of contradicting myself and compromising the adherence to non-dualism in language. There is no benefit for me to try to make my language free of contradictions. By virtue of my contact with 'Sailor' Bob Adamson, the basics are clear. I have no position to maintain, not even of being a non-dualist or being consistent with myself.

So everything that may arise is actually in response to a given question and questioner. It is given to dismantle the question and throw the questioner back upon the recognition of his true being as present awareness. Both the question and answer are dispensed with. Both are false. Once the task at hand is accomplished, both are discarded. Depending on where the questioner is coming from, the discussion of human suffering, for example, will come out entirely differently. For some, you may say it is all the oneness, so do nothing. To another, you will recommend that he trace the root of suffering and dismantle it through clear seeing. At the surface, these suggestions are totally contradictory. It all depends on the situation.

There is no teaching. There is no consistent verbal formula. There are no ultimately 'right' words. Everything that comes out of our mouths is pure bullshit. But the saving grace is that what is being pointed to has nothing to do with words. It is a communication of a non-verbal recognition of being or presence. The words are just the messengers. The real message is the source from which the words are arising. The actual truth to be known is the fact of your own being. Seeing this, there is a relaxation and release of the attempt to 'get it right' in words.

Well this is a lot of words to say that all words are bullshit, including mine! As Bob Adamson says: 'All there is, is non-conceptual, self-shining, ever-fresh presence awareness, just this and nothing else. There is nothing other than this'. The rest is silence. You are that and there is absolutely nothing left to do or know. Finished!

50

Seeing Is the Key, Not Any Action You Take

Question: I have noticed that the concept of time has been one of the things seemingly hard to let go of.

John: Practically speaking, this is not about having to let go of something. This implies someone (a separate entity) to let go and some onerous task to perform. This puts a wrong twist in the equation. It is better just to see the facts of the situation and let the clear seeing have whatever impact it will have. This eliminates the emphasis on a self and a separate doer. For example, just see that time is a concept in the mind. Full stop. Apart from thinking about the past and future, there are no such things. Seeing this clearly, the seeing will pull the energy out of the belief in time as a means to some achievement. The understanding is the transforming factor, not any action taken by an apparent individual.

Q: The issues (the concept of 'I' and time) have become clearer for me, and at times everything is fairly transparent. Then when there seems to be unresolved issues or something still to come, I realize (usually some time afterwards) that it was the process of objectifying things and forgetting the basic issues that lead to the idea of a problem or some future insight (for which I am waiting). So, in a way (and this is just becoming clearer for me as I type this), I can see that the objectifying and the apparent problem are really just one thing.

John: Good seeing. This is clear.

Q: In fact, one of the little buried things that kept 'me' from fully embracing 'What is wrong with right now unless you think about it?' was a shallow understanding of it. I was seeing that yes, you only suffer when thinking about something, but I was still assuming that there was a problem or some actual basis for suffering. Just not thinking about it did not really seem to be a satisfying solution. So, I am seeing now that it is the thinking process that actually creates and is the basis of suffering itself. So, to not buy into the thinking is a perfectly good answer to the apparent problem.

John: Very good that this has become clear. It is a key insight. Once you see that suffering is just a movement in thought and has no real existence, the sword is put to the root. You can never quite experience it the same way once you see this. Again, the seeing is the key, not any action you take—because there is no 'you'!

To take this a bit deeper, you can see that whether suffering thoughts arise or not, awareness is not affected in the slightest. It continues to shine clear and free. The suffering has never touched your real being. From that position, it is immaterial whether thoughts appear or not. Awareness remains untouched. However, as a side effect, the turbulence in the mind tends to subside because the root driver has been exposed. Continue to come back to the inherent, ever-free nature of present awareness. This takes you immediately out of the game.

Q: I guess this should be pretty obvious from reading your book, but there is a difference between being told something and discovering it for yourself. I think I am still in the thick of that process. I really appreciate your support.

John: At some point with all this, the realization simply strikes home that all along you have been nothing but the ever-present, ever-free presence-awareness itself. Since this is here and clearly present already, there is really no process, nor a separate 'I' in the thick of it! However, what you are seeing sounds good. All of this naturally becomes clear as you settle in with it.

51

Seeing Is Enough

Question: Thank you for taking the time to reply to my e-mail. I have spent this past month following on with your recommendation, finding resonance with the natural state of presence-awareness. It is absolutely true that this awareness is always present, best summed up as 'Wherever I go, there I am'. It is also apparent that there is nothing wrong with this unless I think about it.

John: This is key to see. If you stick with what you have seen here, everything is contained in this understanding. Everything else that arises is just an imagined thought in present awareness. It does nothing to your real nature. You are totally free right now. However, when we believe the thoughts, we overlook the natural state of freedom. It is so incredibly simple that we overlook it—for a time!

Q: The confusion arrives when I go looking for an experience.

John: Yes. But then you see that you do not need to do this. It is a 'fool's errand'. With the rising of a sense of 'I' comes in a sense of lack and then the habit of looking for an experience to fulfill that lack. But it is a bottomless pit because the concept of separation is simply not true. It has not happened. There is no lack or problem except as an imagined concept. Seeing the concept as a concept is all the doing that you need. Basically, do not fall for the concept. Just see it as a concept and the seeing dissolves it. Absolutely nothing is gained. You just abide or remain as the natural condition that you have never left.

Q: For instance, I will read 'It is the source of joy, happiness and love'. I will compare my experience with my idea of joy, happiness and love and decide that I am separate from what I think I should be. These thoughts, in turn, result in feeling dissatisfied, which again seems to be proof that I am not there yet. Caught up in the flow of experiences, I miss the fact that none of it is happening outside of awareness. It is a case of 'riding an ox to find an ox'. I guess this is the eternal problem of a seeker.

John: Yes. Just see it all as useless spinning in conceptual thought, in pure imagination. Where is all that appearing? In present awareness, of course. So you are right in the midst of the clarity, even when that is appearing. Again, it is just a matter of seeing what is happening. The seeing is enough.

The seeker does not exist. There is no separate seeker apart from presence-awareness. You already are what you are seeking.

Q: I think the other source of confusion lies in believing all the ideas I have about myself or assuming my individuality to be true.

John: This is true and clearly seen. It is the false notions and ideas that draw the attention into the mind and, seemingly, away from clarity. But this is an illusion, because your being has not gone anywhere.

Q: I do some inquiry into this, but I am not clear on the distinction between what is the living presence-awareness and the idea that I am someone.

John: It is easy to distinguish between awareness and ideas. Just have a look and see that awareness is clear, vivid, alive and doubtlessly present. It is that continuous sense of registering or knowing of all that appears. Ideas are just images, ideas or words arising in the awareness.

Q: I cannot experience it because I am it. This is the impossibility of looking for an experience of myself—and finding frustration.

John: This is not clearly seen. Presence-awareness is bright, fully clear and obvious at all times. I call it 'the ever-present obvious'. Frustration arises because you are imagining it to be something else and thinking it (whatever you are imagining) is not here. It is here (and now) always. It is the simple fact of being, presence, life, awareness.

Q: I think Bob Adamson describes this as an imagined self-centre so close to intelligence-energy that it thinks it is it. Like an iron in the fire, it gets hot and burns like fire, yet take it out and what can it do? So I mix up (in thought) the idea of 'me' with a real living presence.

John: Yes, but at least you are seeing the difference! This recognition will continue to grow until it is completely impossible to confuse your real nature with thoughts about it. You are well on your way to seeing this already.

Q: There have been so many times when the sense of being is all there is. There is just contentment, and then a thought will appear like 'Is this all there is?' or 'Surely there must be something else, after all who do you think you are?' or 'Have you really understood what all those guys are talking about?' Such thoughts come along and turn a feeling of natural well-being and ease into dis-ease and confusion—if I believe them. The habit is that I follow those thoughts as if it is a line of inquiry. But it is plainly more involvement with the mind. But I am reminded that all of this can only ever take place now within awareness.

John: That is the ticket. Once you see the mechanism of what is going on, you are less and less inclined to follow thoughts like that. When the awareness is so bright and clear and available, why invite needless suffering and confusion? Until this was clear, we were operating under a basic ignorance that fueled these habits. When seen, this ignorance is undercut.

Q: Thanks once again for taking the time to reply. I am left with a big inner smile. So it really is that simple, that obvious! I had never slowed down enough to see what is right here and has always been the case until you pointed it out.

I just casually opened the book '*I Am That*' and came across this passage: 'You can find what you have lost. But you cannot find what you have not lost'. That seems to encapsulate just what happens. The premise of a thought, more often than not, is based on finding something that is supposedly lost. The mechanism is exposed. It feels like knowing how the magician performs the trick. It is a very clever illusion!

52

The Thought 'I Am' and the Actual 'I Am'

Question: Is there a difference between the sense of being present (which is there when there is a moment of no thought) and the feeling of 'I am'?

John: The real presence is there always, whether thought is present or not. Your existence does not increase or decrease if thought is present or absent. Do not associate your existence with a quiet mind! Many people make this mistake. I also did at one point. Just remember that the actual 'I am' is that undeniable existence and awareness that is right with you now. The thought 'I am' is just a thought. You exist whether you think that idea or not. What is it that the thought or word 'I am' points to? It is the fact of your own being. You are that.

Q: The sense of being present seems to be there within the body and also without. Does this make sense? However, there is no more mental agitation and no more seeking.

John: When you realize that what we are seeking is the reality of our own natural being and awareness, the seeking falls away, along with the agitation and suffering. All of that was due to the belief that reality was distant and far way. So it was based on a misconception.

Q: It is understood that if it cannot be seen now, then it cannot be sought and found.

John: Yes, what we are seeking is always present. Anything that is not present or can disappear cannot be your true being.

Your own being is the reality. It is not the body, the senses or the mind. These things appear in awareness, which is ever with you. You are that awareness.

53

The Limits of Effort

Question: I have been reading your writings and have a question pertaining to 'right effort'. After twenty years of Vipassana meditation, I 'stumbled' into advaita last year and things began to dissolve rather quickly. Following a session with Tony Parsons last fall, the apple cart really dumped over and I did not sleep for a week. Since that time, I have really resonated with the writings of Nisargadatta Maharaj, Bob Adamson, Gilbert Schultz and especially yourself. Everything seems to be slowing down now and at times almost comes to a complete stop, while life just seems to continue on its own effortlessly (busy job, wife and two young children and so on). I still find myself doing formal meditation each morning, but it no longer has any special significance (other than I am sitting still and breathing).

So, to my question. Obviously, I am still seeking, as I still believe that this body-mind could be gone at any time and one needs to awaken from the dream before it is too late. Do you have any words to help with this apparent dilemma of 'no seeking' versus 'earnestness' (a term Nisargadatta Maharaj used)?

John: Effort is good at one stage, but it will ultimately fall away. It is based on the notion that we are an individual that needs to do something to get 'there'. This is a false concept. Keeping up the effort approach will be self-defeating (actually, self-maintaining!) past a point, since it reinforces the belief in a separate entity. I do not categorically deny effort, but in the end it has some limits. You say:

'Obviously, I am still seeking, as I still believe that this body-mind could be gone at any time and one needs to awaken from the dream before it is too late . Do you have any words to help with this apparent dilemma ... ?'

All these questions and dilemmas I know only too well from my own experience! They all hang on a subtle misunderstanding of our real nature. If you are a separate entity apart from reality, then these questions are troubling. Our very questions and sense of dilemma shows that we are, at some level, still holding onto this notion. However, it can be resolved conclusively by taking a fresh look at things. What is the reality? What is my true nature? Are these truly separate? And this separate 'I' that we take ourselves to be, what is it? Where is it? Can we find it?

A life of suffering presupposes that these questions are not fully clear to us. Once they are understood, the root of suffering, doubts and questions is resolved, and these issues do not trouble us. Until then, the questioning goes on until we are satisfied and see the truth for ourselves.

54

The Sense of Responsibility

Question: Nothing is much of a problem. It is clear to me that there is no doer, no credit taker, no self, no this, no that. However, there is still a subtle problem with doership.

John: I think this is coming a bit too trippingly off the tongue! To truly see that there is no self and all the implications of that would leave no doubts or questions or suffering, for that matter. The initial belief in being a separate someone is the start of all the problems. If there is no self, then who or what would be a doer? Who would be responsible and so on? So this is a deep issue that probably needs a fresh look. The question of the nature of the self is the final question. To conclusively answer this is to resolve all possible problems and doubts because these all stem from a basic unclarity about who we are. In fact, other problems do not really even have to be tackled separately, since the belief in a separate self is the lynch pin of the whole network of questions, doubts and problems.

Q: The problem lies with responsibility.

John: This presupposes someone who is responsible. Duties, actions and tasks are not a problem. Your heart, kidneys, lungs and other bodily functions have been ceaselessly functioning from birth. They have not been troubled by a sense of responsibility for their much-needed work. The trouble comes with the sense of being an 'I' who feels itself to be present and responsible. It is all happening to 'me', or 'I' am doing it. That is the kicker and the real source of the trouble. You will find that everything comes back around to the problematic sense of self at the center.

Q: I have a family to support and this, among other experiences in life, has left me less than dreamy-eyed (even though I can allow everything as a dream.)

John: The body and mind support the family they created! Where does the difficulty come in? There must be some other idea in the picture, such as 'These are taking away my freedom or preventing me from doing other things I want to do'. What is at the root of the problem?

Q: Regardless of what I am told about nobody choosing, about nobody being responsible, I cannot get there from here. I look around and observe entire nations as well as lone individuals affected by the conditions of mindset. India with its poverty and sacred cows becomes a classic example of a no-chooser/no-responsibility attitude.

John: There are certainly choices and responsible decisions being made. That is not a problem either. Whether there is any entity present who is doing the choosing or being responsible is another matter. We think 'I am doing this' and that is where the problem crops up. There is nothing wrong with decisions, responsibilities, thoughts, affairs of nations and so on. There is only one sticking point in the picture and that is a wrong belief in what we are or a wrong identification of our real nature with something it is not. That is the problem. And the resolution of that issue frees up everything—while leaving it all intact and going on just as before. It all gets down to a change in perspective, not any particular change in what is happening. I assure you that choices, actions and all else can and will go on. But the suffering does not need to!

Q: For a moment, let us avoid the doer/deed dualism. Regardless of the body-mind, there is a sense of choosing, of responsibility. Call it phenomenal, dream-like, but even so, one could argue that 'choosing chooses'.

John: Yes, and there is no problem with it. It is only when we refer all this to a self-center with its beliefs and preferences that the trouble starts.

Q: Something is there that has an effect, and this effect is begotten by conditions of mind.

John: All true.

Q: What if I believe that a lack of responsibility causes poor choices through passive mindset or neuronal conditioning. Are you saying that I should instead look at it as no cause and no effect? It all just happens? Whether I believe it or not, it will happen? That is what I cannot get to. That is downright scary!

John: The problem is that we take ourselves to be a separate entity apart from the deeper reality. This is the fundamental mistaken notion. Everything spins from this. Doership, responsibiliy, conditioning, fear—all of it starts up and depends upon a lack of clarity about who we are. And there is no resolution on any of it until the fundamental question is tackled.

Who says you need to get to anything? You are the ultimate reality, but just do not see it clearly yet. Being the reality, which is eternal peace and satisfaction itself, what is there to do—except clear up the idea that you are something else? It is only the imagined separate person who is afraid, because he does not know who he is and his ideas are scaring himself.

Q: It is one thing to talk this talk. It is another to walk the walk. (Yes, I know, another dualism.) Why is it scary? Because the mind can anticipate the future and the roads ahead.

John: But the future is just an imaginary concept and does not truly exist. One peculiar trait that arises upon getting clear on your identity is a nearly complete lack of concern for the past and future.

Q: A 'what-will-happen-will-happen' mindset begets the kind of conditioning that affects nations as well as persons. Hindu India again!

John: You have said it. Those who take themselves to be persons are very concerned with past and future and what will happen. But are you merely a person or something more?

Q: I may have no proof that I will in fact take a less desirable route, but I can look around and see the consequences of various kinds of mindsets or conditionings. As I said, examples abound in both societies and individuals. Those with a certain level of anxiety provide for survival of themselves and others, while those without it just might wind up in the 'Slough of Despond'. In short, why is this apprehensiveness there if it is not for valid survival purposes?

John: The body-mind has a built-in sense of preservation and animal fear, no doubt. But are you the body? All the fears and doubts are for the body-mind. We imagine that is what we are and take on board those fears (and add to them) because we have not seen what we really are.

Q: There is also a question on a practical level. We assume there is a 'reality' unto itself that is not merely an idea within consciousness. It would seem that one ignores biology at his peril. Yes, nobody is there to ignore it, but please pardon this wretched dualistic syntax inflicted upon us.

John: It is all going to get back to what is our assumption of what we are. Are you a mere body-mind or something else? Are you a separate self limited by time and space and subject to change? Is there even a separate self? All problems hang on a fundamental unclarity about this issue. That is the heart of it. And there is no resolve to the mind's problems and dilemmas without clearing this up decisively. Not even pursuing the teachings of non-duality are of much use until the nature of the problem is understood and you find the answers for yourself.

If you want to hone this down to the core and try to get some perspective on things, think over what you take yourself to be. What are you? What ideas do you have about who and what you are. It is the beliefs that we have about ourselves that determine our experience at a practical, day-to-day level.

55

Let the Focus Relax from Thought

Question: This afternoon and this evening I can say that the mind still seems to have exhausted itself, although there has been no opening up to the recognition you describe—of infinity and eternity. The exhaustion derives mainly from an understanding that has grown in the last twenty-four hours that increasingly everything, including the most subtle, is a kind of object, and also that 'I' am always regarded as an object. This regard can be considered as itself nothing more than the momentum of neurons worn into a habitual cycle.

John: The world, the body, the mind and all else arise in awareness. This fact of awareness is who you are. That awareness is what is pointed to as the ultimate reality itself. It is bright, clear, invariable and utterly free of the content that is appearing in it. It is also the source of happiness, joy and love. It (you) is free and always has been free. Not recognizing this, we have imagined ourselves to be a body, a mind or a person. This imagination is the only bondage. In looking to find our sense of self in the appearance, we find there is nothing that can be grasped as 'I'. Thus our entire sense of identity is based on a wrong belief and that is the source or genesis of the problem. This can be cleared up easily and quickly once the true position is pointed out.

Awareness, or your true nature, is not a thing or an object to be grasped by the senses or mind. For this reason the mind is utterly unable to understand what is being pointed out. Yet if I ask you 'Are you aware?' you immediately recognize the presence of awareness or the fact of your own being. True insight does not rely on the mind at all.

Realize yourself to be that awareness in which everything appears. Settle in with that as your identity. This non-conceptual looking will unwind the core misidentification of being a separate 'I'. All of the seeking and searching will fall away and will be replaced with a spontaneous clarity, ease and joy. This cannot leave you because it is your own being. And you cannot lose your own being. You will find that all suffering is created in thought, based on the idea of being something apart from being-awareness. So let the focus relax from thought and simply rest in the bright, open and present awareness that you cannot deny. All speculation and theorizing is a bottomless pit. It is all provisional. Under no circumstances can you doubt your own being, your own presence as awareness. Probe into this through direct, immediate seeing—not thinking. You will discover a depth of peace and certitude that the mind cannot get to via thinking. The answer is not in the mind. It lies in immediate, non-conceptual recognition of the principle of being-awareness, which is what you are. It is effortless, once we stop looking to thought for an answer. See your nature as awareness and not as a separate person.

56

There Is No Answer in the Future

Question: Imaginary or not, we always anticipate the consequences of our actions. We save for a rainy day. We plan what we will do on vacation. Whether the person is concerned or not, there is always an anticipation of what will happen if A is done rather than B—regardless of whether A or B can be chosen. Yes, all Eastern thought advises that the present is that from which everything flows. Still, if we live for today, we may not be happy to see what happens to us tomorrow or a year from now. It is tied in with conditioning, with which you seem to concur in principle, although not in my misconstruction.

John: Obviously at the relative level we plan for the future and learn from the past and so on. This all goes on quite well and is not that much of a problem. From a spiritual or psychological standpoint, things get a bit sticky for the following reasons. When we are unclear on our basic identity and are living under the sway of the feeling of being an independent and isolated self, we are plagued with a fundamental sense of doubt, insecurity and fear. This leads to all manner of questions, seeking, searching, grasping at imagined sources of happiness and so on. At a mental level this manifests as agitated, distressing thoughts and emotions. Rather than getting to the core and resolving the basic source of the problem, many of us attempt to fix the problem by searching for security, certainty and happiness in the world, through the body or through the mind. But the answer is never really fully achieved because we are overlooking the basic root cause of the problem.

Another place where we often look is in an imagined future where 'everything will be all right' and all our problems will be solved. For many of us this imagined future is fraught with incertitude and generates all manner of worry and concern. This is because we are pinning our hopes on finding security and happiness there. However, we are intelligent enough to realize that things may or may not pan out as we desire. But again, we are barking up the wrong tree. There is no particular resolution to the search for happiness in the future, any more than there is in the past or present. All those directions are still looking away from the source of the problem. In fact, if all your energy is going into thinking about the past and future, there is precious little energy available for the inquiry that will lead to a real solution. That is why, from a spiritual perspective, the concept of looking for an answer in the future is a trap. On strictly present evidence, the future only exists as an idea not a present reality. It is hard to conceive that one could locate what is ultimately real in an imaginary idea. The present itself is also an idea, which only has meaning in relation to a past and future. The fact of being or pure awareness is not in the past or future—nor even in the present. These all appear within awareness itself, which is outside of or beyond time. This is where the real answer lies.

57

The Separate Self Is a Fiction

Question: I owe gratitude to you because of your support and because of what you told me. I had written you that recognition will come or it will not and nothing is to be done about it. In effect, you said ignore the 'scholarly' advice and press on.

This phenomenon called the self broke wide open yesterday to reveal itself as an appearance in awareness. It is another appearance like a bird twittering or the refrigerator groaning. Sitting here, typing this, nobody does anything. The mind locates various sensations for purpose of description—ache in knee, taps of keyboard against fingertips, sound of dishwasher, taste of apple. Without the mind, they are unconnected dots, dots forever changing. Connect the dots and—bingo!—there is some kind of secondary effect and the awareness of the secondary effect. Put together enough secondary effects and behold an ego, a self. This, too, occurs in awareness. It and awareness have no shape. They are nowhere. They are no-thing.

I was about to say that this must become clearly recognized, which makes sense from a relative level. Of course, there is nothing to be done. It is happening right now, even as I type. And none of it is forming a single entity—except as another appearance in awareness. This is the natural state. It really is not even a state.

It seems to me that the traditional term of choice, 'awareness', should not be used in any novice primer. The word is a noun, so the seeker goes off in pursuit of something not in motion. 'Awareness-ing' would be a better choice were it not so awkward. All is in process, and the mind can not fixate on any of it. The mind would give up sooner if it understood earlier that it is in an endless loop.

John: With no identifiable separate self in the picture, there is no one present who has a problem, no one who needs to get anywhere, no one who is lacking, deficient or apart. The discovery of the lack of any substantial person or being effectively annihilates all problems, doubts, questions, seeking and suffering. All of these hinge on the belief or assumption of the existence of this separate self and our identity as that. That is a total fiction, an absence, a nothing. Appearances, actions, perceptions, feelings, thoughts, choices and intelligent behaviors all go on spontaneously, just as they always have. Yet they are no longer being referenced to an imagined self-center.

This perspective is obtained through clear seeing and understanding alone—not by someone, but by pure intelligence, pure knowingness itself. No person can ever claim understanding, because the core insight is the recognition of the total absence of anything corresponding to a separate person. However, the root of delusion is removed by clear seeing. And life goes on without the doubt, separation and suffering that was generated in thought by the belief in the existence of a separate self. The error is removed. Nothing else is gained, because the ever-present natural state has never been lost. That awareness, that pure functioning has always been present.

That pure awareness or experiencing shines in and through all states and experiences as that steady, bright and clear presence-awareness that never leaves you. That is what you are, that untouched cognizing emptiness or space-like awareness. All appearances rise and set in that presence that you are. They have no separate existence apart from that and ultimately must be only that, in essence. It is all one substance and that substance is presence-awareness itself, which is what you are. You are completely and fully that now.

Now you are in a better position to understand the statement at the top of my website, which sums things up:

'Our true nature is that simple and undeniable presence of awareness that illumines all thinking, feeling and perceiving. Always present and radiantly clear, it is never obscured by time, circumstances or thoughts. The body, mind and world rise and set in awareness and have no independent existence apart from awareness. Awareness, your real being, is all there is. You are not the limited person you have taken yourself to be. Look for the separate self and you find it entirely absent. Seeing this, suffering, doubt and confusion effortlessly drop away, revealing your natural state of innate happiness and freedom. Understanding who you are is immediate and always available—here and now'.

Now you know this for yourself. Settle in with this understanding and watch a life of doubt and suffering be replaced by steady peace, clarity and certainty. This is what the teachers were pointing at all along. But now it is your living experience, not something based on theoretical knowledge.

What will 'you' do now? This is a false question. Thoughts, feelings and actions will play in the light of awareness, leaving you always free and untouched like the sun in the sky. In the appearance, actions will be taken according to the natural capacities of the body and mind as prompted by the innate intelligence which has been living 'you' from the start.

Q: Thanks for all your help over these months. Off and on through the years and these months there have been moments of depression, even disgust. At such times I had thought this was so much bullshit and I was a great fool. Some teachers I distrusted even though they might be the 'real McCoy'. You, however, represented an honesty and straightforwardness. No bullshit. No bells and whistles. Just the straight dope. Reading and re-reading your material and messages kept me going.

John: Your own interest and commitment to freedom has kept you going. The answers have always been right with us. All the means we ever needed were always within our grasp. Our own innate knowingness is ready to respond once the essentials are pointed out simply and directly. Once the basic position is seen and understood, you cannot lose it. The seeing does not depend on a teacher, a book or anything you get from outside. The seeing is all your own. It is that innate intelligence that has been at work from the beginning. Let your understanding flow from the recognition of the natural state of presence-awareness that you can never leave. Everything is functioning spontaneously in that without any reference to a self-center or any particular reference point or fixed position. You are that natural, free flowing awareness always.

58

Thoughts Do Not Touch You

Question: Things seem to improve and then backslide, improve and backslide. Yesterday morning, following our meeting, the mind began taking me for another ride. Then, I sort of snapped out of it and realized that the thoughts are not me, as I have done before. But there seems to be a persistence of thought, and it seems that it is harder to separate myself from them. These thoughts are particularly troubling. More than anything, I need this to come to an end. This may be beyond the realm of what you would deal with. But if you see anything that could help me, it would be greatly appreciated.

John: If you get into fighting thoughts, judging them, resisting them, condemning them, needing them to drop or be different, then you will come to an impasse. This is all based on a wrong understanding. Never have I or any teachings in the non-duality line ever even suggested doing such things. So somehow, these approaches have been picked up and are still being given some weight. The whole basis of suffering is the mind creating erroneous concepts and beliefs that we then take to be real. Whatever the mind says about you are just some unexamined, erroneous beliefs that were picked up during the years of not knowing any better. None of them are true! They have no real significance in relation to you. And there is not anything that needs to be done. See a thought as a thought and let it be. It will come as it went. When you see thoughts as thoughts and put no particular value or weight on them, they leave. It is like a rude salesman knocking at your door. Ignore him and he leaves.

There is being (your awareness) and thoughts. Put your

attention on the fact of your being and turn away from self-centered thoughts as being irrelevant. Pull the attention away from them and they wither like autumn leaves. Our interest, to the point of excessive focus, is what gives them all the juice. Do not be concerned about a pile of dead, lifeless leaves. As they blow in, they will blow out.

Give up the idea of waiting for a shift or some cosmic realization that will suddenly end the search. The whole idea of a shift or grand attainment is a false concept. See it as false, and in that seeing it will drop away. Anything that can arise in the future is not worth waiting for. What we discover is that present and natural awareness that is here now and effortlessly available. You do not need anything—no event, no grand insight. Leave all these thoughts and concepts alone and rest in and as being, which is a natural and uncomplicated presence that is bright with peace and love. Thoughts do not touch this at all. So do not fight thoughts. Only see them for what they are. If you can turn away from them, do so. If not, then thoroughly question them. You are not a thought. Thoughts do not touch you.

59

You Are Not a Something or Someone

Question: I have noticed that as I get very involved with all kinds of activities there is a heightened sense of doership—'I' am making things happen, 'I' am responsible for what occurs, 'I' need to get it right and so on. This seems to be the opposite of the non-volitional, no-separate-self stance of 'enlightened ones'.

John: There is nothing wrong with doing, thinking, acting or deciding. All of that goes on and will not stop till that body and mind give up the ghost. The 'non-volitional' concept is problematic and tends to generate doubt as it is somewhat vague or abstract. Then we think, 'I am here, but I am not supposed to be consciously doing anything'. But that is confusing and misses the mark. It is far too complicated! There is still a sense of identity, of being a particular entity in the picture. From that position, we are trying to understand and apply the non-dual pointers. But from that position it is not doable or even possible. Thus the frustration.

As always, the issue arises from the relating of all these activities, which are perfectly fine in themselves, to an 'I', a separate being who takes ownership of them. So the sticking point is the referencing of all these things to 'me'. Everything else is, at best, a secondary issue. This issue of the 'me' is the only point that needs clarity. As long as this is not precisely clear, we dance in agony around all the spiritual pointers and teachings. The trouble is that the mistaken identity is still operative and nothing can be clearly understood through the filter of a mistaken 'me' identity.

So I would recommend that you forget all tangential issues

and stick with the basic Question:'Who or what am I?' There are thoughts, feelings, perceptions, actions going on—fine. Are any of these my real nature, my constant identity? If not, then what am I? Tossing all those overboard as 'not I', what is left? Is there a person, entity or thing anywhere in the picture that I can find and say 'This is myself'? I cannot deny my own presence, my own being. But what is it?

All of the conceptual problems hang on my assumed identity as a thing, a body, a person, a thinker, an agent—but am I any of these? All of these depend on the idea that I am something, someone. If I am not a something or someone, then all of those problems have no basis or support. It is the belief in my being something or someone that keeps the whole show in operation.

Everything resolves smoothly when the identity of your true nature is absolutely clearly perceived without confusion. Everything goes on just as before, but the referencing of things to a self-center ceases. Then you stand as what you are and always have been.

60

The Cause of Suffering

Question: You stated that the most effective path is to get to the fundamentals and discover our true nature and remove the cause of suffering. I do understand the fundamentals and rest as 'true nature' often. Removing the cause of suffering is what jumped out at me in your response. That is interesting. Buddhists seem to talk of the removal of suffering a lot. I take it that the cause of suffering is identifying as the individual who thinks, instead of maintaining the position of identifying as true nature, in which the thinking mind shows up in. Could you say more on the removal of suffering?

John: Step one is to see that all suffering, problems, doubts and questions arise in thought and nowhere else. There is nothing inherently wrong 'out there' nor in the body or mind themselves. Suffering is a creation in thinking. See if that is clear. Then we can go on to the next step.

Q: Step one is very clear. What is step two?

John: While suffering appears or is created in thinking, not all thoughts generate suffering. For example, thinking '2 + 2 = 4' does not generally cause much of a problem. Most of the thoughts in the mind are just practical and impersonal and do not trigger anxiety or suffering. So if you are going to track down the root cause of suffering you must be precisely clear on what type of thoughts trigger anxiety and suffering. Can you identify for yourself those types of thoughts that generate the most concern? I am looking for a broad category or bucket into which most suffering thoughts can be grouped.

Q: The broad category or bucket that generates the most concern is thoughts about I, me.

John: Yes. Self-centered thoughts are what suffering is—nothing else. You are that unchanging awareness which is already free, and there is nothing to obtain or do regarding that fact. The very sense of being and awareness that is easily and doubtlessly present is what you are.

Now, whenever self-centered thoughts appear, there is the arising of apparent suffering. Suffering means any type of worry, anxiety, fear, doubt, question, problem, seeking and so on. Be clear—I am not talking about physical pain or ordinary bodily reactions. Nor am I talking about natural and spontaneous feelings and emotions coming through.

One key thing to note is that the appearance of self-centered thoughts does not actually disturb presence-awareness. In fact, those thoughts only arise in the light of that awareness. So you never lose your true nature under any circumstances. The thoughts arise and set in presence-awareness (you) and leave you clear, free and undisturbed at all times.

However, it is still worthwhile to thoroughly understand the origin and mechanism of suffering. Self-centered thoughts have been acquired over the course of living. They live and survive in thought. Without thought they are not existent. This leads some people to attempt to suppress or get rid of thought entirely. But this response is based on an incomplete analysis of the matter—a case of throwing the baby out with the bath water.

So continue to trace these thoughts to their ultimate cause. What is the cause of the self-centered thinking? What is the root of it? In other words, what must be necessary to allow the creation and survival of self-centered thoughts?

Q: Thanks for your last response. It was very refreshing to read it. You asked 'What is the source of the self-centered thoughts?' My answer is that it seems to be from a false sense of 'me'. A false 'I', based on memories from the past that are continuously dragged into the present and pollute the present with this false sense of 'me'.

John: Yes. You are seeing this clearly. So, self-centered thoughts are rooted in the assumption or belief that there is a substantially existing thing called a self. This is otherwise called an ego, a person, an entity or, as you have said, a sense of 'me'. Not only is this self assumed to be real or present, but even more importantly in terms of the experience of suffering, we believe that this is what we are. In other words, all suffering depends on the belief in a substantial, existing self. All of the self-centered thoughts are really just attributes or definitions of this entity. They have accumulated over the course of time. The arising of this belief in a separate self and our identity with that is the origin of suffering, doubt and the general sense of confusion about ourselves. All the subsequent self-centered thinking has been an attempt by the mind to define this uncertain sense of self. However, the whole network of self-centered thoughts and identities only added more confusion. It has obscured the basic issue to the point that we have become unable to see the core mechanism at work. Without exposing this core mechanism fully and clearly, all efforts to rid ourselves of suffering are doomed to fail. This includes all forms of practice, doing, seeking, renouncing, meditating, indulging—or any of their opposites.

Now, seeing that the whole network of suffering is based on the belief in the presence of a separate self and our assumed identity with that, the solution is going to be to look to see if we can discover any such thing that is, in fact, a separate self. Can I find anything, anything at all, about which I am prepared to say 'This is myself. This is who I am'? In other words, if this self-center exists and is real, I should be able to find it. Have a look into your thoughts, feelings, perceptions and anywhere else in your experience and see if you can find something that you can grasp hold of and say 'This is me'. See if you can find this self-center, which we have seen to be the root of all of our suffering.

Q: I cannot find a self-center. The sense of 'me' is a false self.

John: The most important fact to glean from this is that when you investigate the cause of suffering, you discover that it does not exist. Therefore, suffering is an appearance in the mind based on a false assumption. It survives as long as the cause (the separate self) is assumed or imagined to be real. If the cause is questioned and found to be non-existent, then can the effects remain? For example, when you imagine a thief in the house, there may arise fear and various plans to deal with the situation. But when you investigate and see that there is no thief can those fears and thoughts remain? To see for your-self—not as a theory, but as a result of direct looking—that there is no separate self pulls the root out of the whole net-work of self-centered thinking or suffering. What remains is the clear, doubtless presence of awareness, which is your natural state. With this recognition arises an innate sense of happiness, clarity and freedom which you cannot lose, since it is your own true being. And you cannot lose your own be-ing, your own presence. In the absence of any self-centered thoughts, the direct understanding of who you are remains clear, unwavering and free of doubt.

Q: There seems to be an awaring going on even when I lie down to sleep.

John: Yes, awareness, which is your sense of presence or existence is going on as the continuous support or background of all appearances or states.

Q: Self-centered thoughts arise in awareness.

John: Yes. But now you know that these are based on a false belief and only survive due to this false belief. Once the belief is exposed, these thoughts do not bind you. Furthermore, when the energy of belief no longer goes into them and you settle in with the recognition of your real nature, the self-centered thoughts tend to naturally fall out of the picture. But whether and when this happens is of no real consequence because the awareness is what you are anyway. That is not touched by the appearance of thoughts.

Q: I try to continuously identify as awareness and not the self centered thoughts of a temporary 'me'.

John: Who is the 'I' that is trying to identify as awareness? This is still a self-centered thought, albeit very subtle! You are awareness. You do not have to identify with what you already are! Just come back to the core insight that these thoughts refer to a self-center that is not real or existent. Still, you cannot deny your actual being-awareness. And are you separate from that at any time? Seeing that, there is no need to identify with something from which you cannot be separate. Simply see the true facts. That seeing is enough.

Q: At times I feel like a yo-yo, flipping from identifying as awareness and then identifying as the self centered thoughts of a time-bound 'me'.

John: These are just thoughts arising and setting. Look directly into your presence as awareness. This will provide a steady vantage point. Your being does not come and go. Do not try to dis-identify with self-centered thoughts by an act of will. Who would do such a thing? Awareness is already free of thought. Just see a false concept as false. Self-centered thoughts may appear, but they are groundless and do not refer to anything substantial. As they come, so they will go—easily and effortlessly. You remain as you always are—that ever-free presence-awareness, which is your true identity. You do not achieve it, you recognize that this is what you are and always have been. Seeing this, the self-centered thoughts take care of themselves without any need for a technique or process to deal with them. A life free of suffering is discovered as your natural state.

Now You Know

Question: It may be just my imagination, but your articles seem to be getting more and more 'on the mark', hitting the nail on the head more and more directly, driving it home with more and more precise pointers. I needed you, John. But not anymore! Thank you so much.

John: Thanks for the note. It is always nice to hear when the pointers click. The more you settle in with this, the clearer the pointers seem to get. That was my experience. They are clearest of all when you realize you are beyond the need of pointers! Now this is your undeniable experience. The beauty of this is that everything you need is present within you, even from the start. All false concepts, practices, reliance on time, reliance on others—everything—is exposed as irrelevant to the basic understanding which is always immediate and clearly available. There is no one that can deny the fact of present awareness and their identity with that. Now you know.

The Body and Mind Are Not Impediments

Question: Help, John! I must still be lost in the realm of the ego after all? I have noticed that there remains an underlying compulsive quality to my experience, a gnawing restlessness and a subtle sense that things are still not OK in certain respects. This seems to revolve mainly around my two main life goals, which I feel have thus far eluded me. These are the search for a fulfilling and financially rewarding career and the desire for a loving relationship. The latter is also linked with the strong biological craving for sexual satisfaction.

This manifests most obviously as the seemingly futile obsession over trying to solve my career dilemma and looking for love behind every door and what seems the equally futile obsession of trying to figure out how to create some romance in my life. It becomes particularly consuming on my days off, when I have nothing particular to do. There is not much else I really want to do except relax and enjoy life as it is. But instead, I just find myself sitting around my apartment, plagued by the sense that I should be constantly doing something to get these needs met (like a little voice saying, 'Time's a wastin' and you ain't gettin' no younger!').

I have been waiting for my true nature as pure awareness to dissolve this inner drama and compulsive searching, but since it does not appear to be happening, I thought it would be a good idea to run it by you and see where I may be going astray. Also, I still have yet to read any of your writings where you directly address the question of how the sex drive is integrated in presence-awareness, so I will be very interested to see what you have to say about this.

John: All the relative issues come into balance as the basic understanding of who you are sinks in. In fact, there is not much attention that goes into them except the common sense responses to any given situation. The compulsive fixation on outcomes and things being a certain way definitely lessens. We get into these patterns because the mind is convinced that our happiness is riding on the outcomes of these events. It really is not, so we need to look a bit deeper to discover the real and abiding source of fulfillment and the root cause of suffering. You can see that all the compulsive thoughts and desires are being generated in thought in response to certain ideas and expectations that the mind sets up.

Of course there are basic physiological and practical components at work, like the sex drive, the need to eat, pay rent and so on. These are practical needs and are best addressed at a practical level. The body needs to eat, craves companionship, needs a place to live and so on. Such is its lot in life! The problem comes in with the identification that 'this is me', 'this is who I am', 'this is important to my sense of self' and so on. It is the relation of these normal experiences to 'I' which associates impersonal events with self-centered thinking. And here arise the problems, questions, doubts and suffering. But I stress that this is not because of the events, but rather the identification with them. When I met Bob Adamson and discovered what he was pointing to, I did not get any particular answers or solutions to my relative life situation at all. Nothing really changed outwardly. However, the belief in the separate self center ceased and, along with that, the habit of relating everything to this false reference point.

So we need not wait around for problems to be magically dissolved. Instead we can look at the root cause of what it is that is generating the sense of there being a problem at all. This does not depend on circumstances being a certain way. If you take that approach, you will wait forever. You are waiting at a painted door, expecting it to open and yield the answer.

Let the body and mind function naturally. They have an inherent intelligence and can take care of themselves. Knowing who you are is not going to magically get you a job or get you a partner! Nothing is going to drop out of the sky if you are sitting around waiting for awareness to 'fix everything'. I recommend using basic common sense and developing job skills or dating skills if needed. I do not think one gets too many romantic opportunities sitting around on the couch!

I can also guarantee that none of these issues are a problem when you have discovered your real nature and uncovered the root cause of suffering.

Q: Thank you very much for your time in offering me some further pointers in my inquiry and sharing from your own personal experience. It has helped in highlighting the key issues. Yes, I am clear that it all comes back to the fundamentals and that once you realize that the separate self is a false assumption (as the cause of suffering) that none of the issues I cite are seen as 'problems'. I also see where you are coming from when you talk about using the 'common sense' approach as being the best way to address one's goals at that level, and that my mistake has been waiting around for awareness to dissolve these issues.

To be honest, John, it seems to me that my real dilemma at this level is that I have reached a point where I really do not even want to be concerned with getting a better career, finding a compatible partner and so on. However, the physiological (for lack of a better word) drive persists of course, which seems to set up a conflict between resting in my true nature and the sense of urgency in dealing with my survival needs. I guess this is why at one time the idea of living out my days in a Zen monastery seemed so appealing to me. But I chose not to pursue it, as my intuition made me realize that until I had directly apprehended my true nature (and knew beyond the mental level that 'this is not me'), that this approach would just represent an attempt to run away from that apprehension.

Having said all that, it seems that there is a paradox here creating a seeming (probably illusory) resistance between recognizing the obviousness of what I am and accepting 'what is' at the practical level. I hope I have not confused you more with my words. I am sure you will be able to help me cut through to the heart of the matter. Meanwhile, like I said before, you have definitely lit my fire!

John: There is no doubt that urges for sex, food, shelter and other things continue. As I see it, they are par for the course for the body and mind. If they are not judged, evaluated or identified with, they can be dealt with pretty easily as part of the natural functioning. Trying to suppress the natural functioning creates its own problems and conflicts. It is kind of like trying to still the mind—you are setting yourself up for failure, because it is practically impossible. I do not have any magic bullets or tricks up my sleeve.

Realize that resting in your true nature does not have to do with having a still mind or not experiencing the desires and interests of the body and mind. Refraining from sex does not bring you any nearer to knowing your true nature, nor does having sex. Either way, you are present and aware and that is what is to be known, in spite of whatever else is going on. Nisargadatta Maharaj said you can realize your true nature in the middle of a battle field. So there is hope for us! My advice is to be bland and relatively unconcerned with these issues. Deal with them to the best of your ability as they arise and then forget them. Keep intent on the core understanding, the core points. What is true? What is your relationship with that? What is suffering? How is it removed? Everything falls into place if you keep to the basics.

I never actually worked out any of these types of relative issues as a special undertaking. By getting clear on the basics, everything has a way of taking care of itself. Part of the problem is defining the situation as being a problem. That comes in based on the point of view or evaluation of the situation. If something is not defined as a problem by the mind, then can you say that it is a problem? The sex drive is the sex drive. It may be weak or powerful. You may act on it or not. Presence-awareness does not really care, does it? And none of that prevents you from understanding what needs to be understood. It is absolutely not an impediment. If it seems to be, then it is the mind defining it as such, but it is not a problem in reality. As long as you are alive, the body and mind will have their actions, desires and states. It is better to come into harmony with the natural functioning than battling it or defining it as a problem.

Even in the midst of desire or thought, have you left awareness or presence? Then how can those things prevent you from resting as your own being? Look clearly and you will understand that this is actually not possible.

63

Mind, Ignorance and Grasping

Question: It is a long time since last I wrote to you. Thank you for continuing your articles. They are strong reminders. Reading your words 'true insight does not rely on the mind at all' I saw the impulse of the mind to understand. It turns on and on hoping that in the end, at some point in the future, it will understand. What futility!

John: It is good that you are seeing this. Seeing is always the key, not anything you do. Now that you know the answer is not in the mind, it frees up the looking to check out some more productive avenues. Leave the mind alone and let it handle what it is good at—practical matters.

Recognizing things like love, awareness or being does not come via the mind. These are always direct and non-conceptual. If this seems nebulous, just ask yourself whether or not you exist or are aware. That obvious and clear recognition is completely non-mental. So it is not difficult. In fact, it is easy. It is so easy that we gloss over it.

Q: I have the feeling that the mind must reach the point of exhaustion in order for it to let go.

John: Not at all. Just use intelligence and clear seeing. Do you need to be exhausted to drop a red-hot iron poker? There is no need to wear out the mind as a prerequisite to understanding. That is just another mental ploy. Just see that the mind is not the right tool for the job and stop using it in these matters. It is more just a matter of clear seeing. There are no other requirements or qualifications needed.

Q: The world as I understand it is a matter of grasping isn't it?

John: Not as I see it. Grasping is an effect of a deeper cause—the search to know what is real and true and what is the source of happiness. Grasping is a misguided attempt to find these things. Once the basics are cleared up, the grasping quality necessarily drops away. As long as there is ignorance and suffering the mind continues to search for an answer. When the answer is believed to be in the body, mind or world, grasping naturally arises. Trying to eliminate grasping without understanding the deeper causes at work is an exercise in futility.

The cause of suffering is not grasping. Rather it is ignorance, a basic unclarity about who we are. From this lack of understanding arises a false sense of 'I'. Then comes all types of identifications and beliefs to try to make this self-center more secure and solid. Self-centered thoughts are the very definition of suffering itself. Due to this mind-created suffering, we naturally experience the desire to be happy, whole and complete. Then comes the pursuit of various things we believe will bring happiness. This leads to grasping and attachment.

If we look for a solution by trying to stop grasping at its own level, the efforts are not going to be effective because the root causes are still at work. It is like cutting the limbs off of a tree. As long as the root is alive, the tree will sprout forth again. But if you clear up the confusion at its source and uproot the fundamental ignorance (belief in a separate self), all the rest of the effects (self-centered thoughts, suffering, seeking and grasping) will naturally fall off without any additional effort.

Q: Thank you for your answers. I find them very useful because they reveal the underlying wrong assumptions of my questions.

John: This all gets down to clearing away any remaining

wrong beliefs and assumptions. This leaves what you are very clear and directly known. Let all this resonate and feel free to stay in touch.

64

You Already Are What You Are Seeking

Question: The insight that 'I am all that is' has resonated very strongly with me lately. It seems to resolve all my philosophical problems, except the state of deep sleep. This has become something of a Zen riddle, like 'What was your face before you were born?' This has lead me to investigate a variety of books and teachings in order to try to get some answers. However, the result is that I am now feeling that the understanding I seek is way beyond where I am now. It seems to have something to do with consciousness without an object. What next?

John: It sounds like you are off searching for the answer! The more you search, the more complicated it gets. This is because any search takes you immediately away from obvious and clear presence-awareness. Any search can only be done by and in the mind, and the answer is not in the mind. That in you which is presently aware of thoughts, experiences and objects is exactly what so-called 'consciousness without an object' is. You are already that and do not need to know it or find it. There can be no perception, feeling or thought without you being present. That presence, which is what you are, is naturally and easily available. It is clear, open and brightly aware. It cannot be known by the mind or thought because thinking appears in or on the awareness that you are. You know the mind. But the mind cannot know you. This is actually very simple if we do not complicate it unnecessarily.

Suffering comes in when we try to define or limit ourselves in terms of the ideas and conceptions in the mind. None of them are true. Everything the mind has tried to say about us is false simply because the mind cannot cognize your true nature of being, presence or awareness (which are different words pointing to the same thing). The belief in being something separate from presence-awareness is the root of all problems. All the subsequent self-centered thinking was just an attempt by the mind to describe this imagined pseudo entity.

Presence-awareness is the answer. It is obvious, evident and known. You cannot doubt your own presence, your own awareness. Nor can you ever say you are separate from it. So all attempts to search for it are bound to fail and they always come up short. You cannot find or understand what you are. You can only be what you are. Just rest in and as the simple and undeniable being-awareness that is the constant background of all experiencing. Let go of the mind's questions, doubts and attempts to define what you are. Two points are important to consider. First, the mind can never know what is being pointed to. Second, the answer is not in the mind. Realize that the mind can never find what you are. You already are what you are seeking.

Q: I believe the answer is not in the mind! But I also believe the mind can help in pointing to the answer. I believe there is something beyond the mind that is deeper and results in more profound changes than I have experienced. There are too many descriptions of profound changes for me to settle for less.

John: Just remember that the key is to look at your own direct experience. Continue with looking and exploring what you can see and verify for yourself. You can discover what in you is beyond thinking, how suffering arises, what alleviates it and so forth. All the workings of this are constantly being displayed in each moment of your experience. Reading about all this is good, but it is all second-hand accounts. When we try to understand what others are talking about, it tends to divert us into conceptual thinking rather than non-conceptual look-ing and understanding of our immediate experience. Reading is not a bad thing, but you need to be aware of its limits. In the end, you see that no book can give you the direct experi-ence of your own being. Just like no map is the territory, no description of being, awareness, peace, oneness and so on are those things. Often, the multiplicity of words, concepts and pointers can mask the simplicity of what is being pointed to.

65

What Is Clear Seeing?

Question: I have been reading some of the articles on your website and notice that you refer to 'clear seeing' at times. What does this mean and how does it work?

John: There is nothing fancy or mystical about clear seeing. It just means to check things out for yourself. Have a look and try to verify what is being pointed out. Do not think about all this too much or analyze it from the perspective of previous beliefs and concepts. Set aside beliefs and assumptions and have a fresh look at your actual experience without reference to ideas and opinions. Use your direct and immediate awareness to see and understand for yourself.

Q: Thanks so much for your response. Everything makes so much sense and really resonates with me. The first problem I encountered was where you said in one of your articles: *'Awareness, your real being, is all there is. You are not the limited person you have taken yourself to be. Look for the separate self and you find it entirely absent'.*

Given my current 'programming', all there is to see, for me, is a separate self. I have come from mainstream religion, through being 'spiritual but not religious' and all that. It has finally dawned on me that, in order to see real oneness, I will need to discard the notion that I am a spirit on my own. I do not have a separate vibration and aura? I am not an eternal spark of cosmic energy with my own destiny on my own journey through what we term 'eternity'? This appears to be what will have to change in order for a separate self to be absent. Is this the correct view?

John: The teachings of non-duality point out that you never have been a separate person or being apart from the single divine source. That source is pure being-awareness. When you look deeply into yourself, you find that you are also only being-awareness. Call it source, spirit, the divine, consciousness—they are just words pointing to that which you are. Everything that appears is just an appearance in and on that.

Q: I guess it is my religious and other spiritual mindset, but I always pictured a separate spirit-self (invisible to human eyes) to be about the size of a piece of rice, with a colored aura denoting what evolutionary level I am on. It seems very silly now to think that we could be reduced to such an entity (which I thought came from the 'big bang'). I see that this would be separateness. For me, that is going to be a little difficult to get over, which is where I suppose clear seeing will help. However, the idea of no separate spiritual-substances does make things completely equal for everyone with no hierarchies of those doing better or worse.

John: The basic delusion is the belief that we are separate independent entities. We imagined we were. If you think you are a separate self, try to find it. You will find that there is no such entity at all that you can grab a hold of or locate.

Q: OK, I can see that. I just thought we all had our own little separate 'rice-sized' pieces of spirit. This is going to be difficult to get past. It is very ingrained and is what I believed I was experiencing—all one in unity of consciousness, but separate in actual experience. I can locate that, picturing it in my mind, but that is probably what needs to drop away. I can see that this all involves the mind.

John: You can see that that imaginary idea is not you. It is just an idea. When you actually look, you do not find any actual thing that is a separate entity at all. So it is a fiction. That is why Christ said, 'I and the Father are One', the Hindus say, 'Thou Art That', and the Buddhists say, 'Your own mind is the Buddha'. God, the individual soul, and the world are concepts that only follow if the belief in being a separate self or ego is accepted. When investigated, that belief is discovered to be false. So are all the other concepts that depend on that false belief.

Q: You have also mentioned in one of your articles the idea of reincarnation. You do not seem to be either pro or con. I began to believe this idea was true when I read various books that documented cases of children who were born with certain 'marks' or 'scars' that corresponded to 'death wounds' from a past life they remembered. Another reason I want to understand clear seeing better is because I have some very resistant traumas that have caused chronic illness and disability, and I believe this could help in my recovery. I definitely have seen past lives for myself with traumatic experiences, so whatever you can point me to about that will be appreciated.

John: You will find in the end that the key lies in seeing that what we are seeking we already are. We are complete and full to perfection. It is all wrong concepts and ideas that we picked up that are the source of our suffering. Seeing this, those false ideas drop away, and we abide in and as the natural state that is our true birth right.

Q: Is there a part of the physical brain-mind that might not accept this for a long time and might have the ability to hold me back from the recovery I seek in actual experience?

John: There is nothing and no one that can prevent you from full realization of what you are. You actually already are what you are. You are present and aware. That presence-awareness is the true nature to be realized. If I ask you, 'Are you present?' 'Are you aware?' you know this already. When you answer 'yes' to those questions, what you are recognizing is your true nature—the simple fact of being itself. The key is that we did not recognize this, nor understand it. So the mind created a false identity of thoughts and concepts. That is all suffering is. The sky is always free of the clouds. You, as presence-awareness, were and are always free of the limiting thoughts and experiences created by the mind. You are not a limited, suffering person. You do not need time or qualifications to see what you are, only a willingness to look and find what was not noticed. There is no purification or practice in this approach. It relies on clear seeing, which just means getting a clear pointer to the basic facts and verifying them for yourself. Your true nature is ever-free, perfect, whole and complete. All the dramas and traumas never touched you. You just imagined you were something you were not. That imagination can end now by simply seeing it was never true.

Q: Wow. I get it! Now I just need to experience it as it sinks in well. I have one more question, but I am going to get the answer myself, then I will let you know. Thanks very much for your patience and availability to help.

John: Let all this percolate. Feel free to stay in touch if any questions come up. Try to keep to the basics and look at your own direct experience for answers. Everything you need is right with you. My blurb at the top of the website covers all the fundamentals as I see them, including what is your nature, how it relates to everything else, where suffering comes from, and how it is eradicated. Everything else I point to and talk about is just a commentary on that. And even that is just a pointer, in words, to the fact of your real nature. Remember—the presence-awareness is clear, open and already present. Spiritual understanding is just a change in perspective, a recognition of something already present but overlooked—till now.

66

Nobody Here, Just This

Question: After extensive communication between us, you may recall that once before, some months ago, I said 'I got it!' only to have it slowly ebb away. The second time, quite recently, however, it took. The mind now does what it has always done, but without any vested interest in its outcomes. It continues on auto-pilot, as always, but without the illusion of a navigator. There is only this openness.

Interestingly, the decisive moment came after covering ground that I thought had been well-traversed. With some it has to do with settling into the seeing. With others it has to do with an 'earth-shaking' recognition. With me, it had to do with reason. The head had to be convinced. The problem was that I thought it had been convinced long ago. No self? Why of course, who can doubt it? No mind? Why, that too.

I suspect that at least some of the problem has to do with the verbal. 'Trippingly off the tongue' was how you responded to some of my more glib expressions, borrowing Hamlet's phrase with the Murder of Gonzago players. By verbal, I mean that I am inclined to be that way as are, no doubt, many of your correspondents. Words fill in ahead of recognition, supplying the 'yeah, I know that' reaction. I discovered that experience can be pigeon-holed without even knowing it.

There were traces of self left. They were subtle and occurred almost unconsciously. Once these were noticed, reason took over. One, as thoughts, they are objects. Two, as objects they cannot be 'me'. Three, they were created. Four, then I cannot find 'me', the creator, anywhere. Then comes along five—give it up mind, you are played out. What the hell more do you want? Six, there it is, the source of all this puzzlement.

Yes, this awareness is so obvious. It precedes all else. There is nothing but awareness and presence in it. Even as I type, these words arise from it. There is nobody here, just this. Thoughts—they, too, are its creatures, always there ahead of recognizing them. I am nothing but air, so to speak.

The radical understanding is that awareness creates all in play, for lack of a better term—these words, these thoughts, that tree, that bird song. There is real pleasure in it all, from the music on the radio to the light in the window, and the pleasure is part of the play.

John: Beautifully said. It is nice to hear how things have settled in. As I always say, your own experience is its own confirmation. There is nothing to add to that! Stay in touch. I would enjoy hearing from you if anything comes up to express.

67

I Cannot Get Over How Easy It Is

Question: I just wanted to let you know things appear to be settling in well here, and tell you how it is manifesting for me. Like many of the people who have communicated with you, I cannot get over how easy resting in one's true nature is! Sometimes I will think, 'There has to be a catch to this', but then almost immediately comes the response, 'A catch for whom?' Then I might start worrying if I am going to lose this insight, and again comes the answer, 'Who is there to lose what? Do I not exist? Can I ever be separate from the awareness that I am?' I even see that whenever thought kicks in and I start spinning stories in the mind, I am pretty quick to dismiss the whole thing as pure nonsense, knowing that this has nothing to do with what I am. My new motto is 'If it's thinking, then it ain't what I am'. Wow, what a difference from the way I was beating myself up just a couple of weeks ago!

The questions are all but non-existent. What you constantly say about all questions and doubts being for the mind only is sinking in. Thoughts seem to evaporate as quickly as they come. The challenges in my daily life continue to be absent of that gnawing, compulsive quality. It is becoming ever more clear that these things at the relative level have nothing to do with what I am fundamentally. I am enjoying the simple things in life again much more. I have much more energy available to deal with things. I notice that these relative issues really do take care of themselves pretty much automatically if you just allow them to! I am also even seeing how concepts like birth, death, pain, suffering, time and consciousness, are really just ephemeral concepts. I can see that presence-awareness (while providing the space for all concepts to arise in) is not a concept. Life just unfolds naturally and takes care of itself without a 'me' needing to do anything (and there is no 'me' there anyway!).

Abiding in pure awareness stripped of identification with concepts and false ideas is joyful and effortless. I have lost my desire to read any more spiritual books and books on self-development (and that is saying a lot, given that seeking until now has been my favorite pastime). I am just re-reading your book and website again to stay grounded in the fundamentals. There just does not seem to be any more to say after that! Thank you again for your uncompromising clarity, John. Stay well and happy.

John: What you are seeing and saying sounds very solid and clear to me. Excellent. The 'acid test' is the freedom from the compulsive and binding quality of conceptual thoughts. The sense of ease and natural freedom is a good sign and shows that this is all taking effect, not as intellectual understanding, but as your direct and immediate experience.

68

In Awareness, There Is No Problem

Question: Last time we talked you suggested that I just stay with presence-awareness and not go in the direction of thought. You said that when this got clear for me then we could talk about the source of suffering.

I have been doing what you suggested and two things have become clear. First, I exist within this presence-awareness. This simple, open space includes this body-mind as well as all the thoughts, emotions and sensations that arise. Included in this is the thought 'I'. It appears true that the 'I' thought often refers just to this body-mind but, in seeing this, it is looking clearer and clearer that the body-mind functions on its own! The 'I' is an afterthought, so to speak. This functioning is happening and then the thought occurs, 'I am thinking', 'I am doing' and so on. Funnily enough, just in watching this it is becoming obvious that suffering is directly tied to belief or investment in the thinking that is occurring and the belief in an 'I' that is doing the thinking. But always, always, always (did I mention, always!?) is the awareness of the thinking, feeling, doing or sensing. And that is always prior to the thinking, feeling, doing or sensing. Or should I say that those things are always arising within this simple, neutral knowing. There has never been a time when the awareness was not there—even at those times I think I have lost awareness. It has never happened. So this body-mind comes after awareness and functions within awareness. Awareness includes the body-mind.

This is very weird and very natural and—suddenly—very obvious. All the regular events continue rolling along, but they are less and less of a problem. The problems only arise as thought. Minus thought, there is just this to do, that to do and so on. It is nothing very dramatic and yet completely different. Even the thought 'Oh, this will not last' is seen as arising in this clear, open space of awareness. It has been very helpful to keep asking, 'And what sees that thought? What feels that sensation? What is aware of that emotion?'

Is this making sense to you? I am a little—more than a little—stunned that it has become so clear. But no matter what arises, it is all seen by this simple presence-awareness right now, right here. And in this awareness, there is no problem, no suffering, no confusion. All of that stuff belongs 'over there' with thinking, with the mind. Suffering and difficulty comes with the seeming forgetting of awareness. And yet it is presence-awareness knowing the seeming forgetting or confusion or mental constipation! This knowing is completely and absolutely reliable 100% of the time! What has happened? I have no idea!

John: Your own seeing and understanding is blossoming. The simple and obvious truth of what is being pointed to starts to kick in. We may resist it for a while, but then the simplicity of it eventually overwhelms the doubts of the mind. From the point of view of the mind, the breath of freedom often comes as an unexpected surprise. The direct recognition of your true nature is not something that the mind can really get a handle on. As far as thought is concerned, what is being pointed to (and which you are seeing for yourself) is 'nothing'. And yet from the perspective of direct, non-conceptual experience, presence-awareness is the most natural and obvious fact of our experience. Without that, we could have no perception, thought, feeling or other experience.

Now your identity as that presence-awareness is becoming clear. And this translates as clarity, peace and freedom. These are things that cannot be manufactured by the mind. Continue to rest in and as this undeniable presence-awareness and discover the treasures inherent in this, your true nature. With this recognition, all the pointers and teachings will have served their purpose. You will simply live in and as that natural state of peace and freedom that is your birth right.

69

You Are the Natural State

Question: I re-read the articles on your website and in your book as well. I pondered the questions you recommended that I look into in your last e-mail, too.

John: What is the truth being pointed to?

Q: The truth being pointed to is that awareness is. Awareness is now. Awareness is untouched by thoughts, feelings, sensations and objects. All happens in awareness.

John: What is your relationship with that?

Q: I am awareness. Without awareness nothing is.

John: What is suffering and where does it come from?

Q: Suffering is thinking. Thinking about bad things that happened to me in the past and thinking about bad things that might happen to me in the future. Thinking about how to fix what is or might be.

John: What is the root cause of suffering and how is it eradicated?

Q: The root cause of suffering is believing that the thoughts and images about me and my story are who I am. Believing that the image, the thoughts, the story, the feelings are what I am, more thoughts are generated to fix the perceived problems. The effort to fix the images, thoughts and so on creates mental, emotional and physical suffering. When it is seen that I am not the thoughts, images and so on and that I am the awareness of all that is, the self-centered thinking is no longer necessary to support or fix the perceived problems of the imaginary 'me'. The absence of the belief in the imaginary 'me' and the self-centered thinking is the relief of suffering.

When there is no self-centered thinking, I know myself as awareness. As awareness I have no past, no future. I am as I am, always now. As awareness, I can not suffer. Suffering requires thought, imagination, past and future.

OK! Right now and as I was pondering your questions, I feel that I am awareness. There is peace. This recognition of knowing myself as awareness and the resulting peace seems to be happening more.

John: Good. Inquiring into the roots of suffering will unwind it all. The fact that you are experiencing more peace is a good sign that this is working effectively.

Q: But why isn't this recognition and the resulting peace experienced always as my natural state?

John: You are the natural state. When the attention wanders into self-centered thinking, we tend to overlook our identity as the natural state. It is that simple.

Q: I have been watching what happens when this peace is lost. There are many thoughts that trigger the self-centered thinking and the suffering.

John: This is good. Make this very practical and hands on. Self-centered thinking is suffering. If you really want to ace this quickly and directly, look into the question 'What is the root and cause of self-centered thinking?' If self-centered thinking has a root cause and you eradicate it, could there be any more effects?

Do not lose sight of the fact that you are present and aware. That is the natural state and you never deviate from it. All we are doing at this point is clearing away any remaining overgrowths of concepts and false ideas. But the essential position is already in effect.

70

The Sun and the Clouds

Question: I do not know that I actually have a question. Perhaps you will detect it in what I am saying. The apparent habitual mind seems to regularly obscure the ease of being-awareness just as a cloud obscures the sunlight.

John: Yes, but only seemingly. Notice that, in fact, your being or awareness is not actually obscured. It is more that the focus is drawn to the thoughts and your true nature is just overlooked. The cloud and sun analogy is good, but take it further and see that the sun (from its own point of view) is never obscured by the clouds. You are the sunlight of awareness. No matter how many thoughts appear, they only appear in awareness.

Q: A feeling of discomfort creeps in and one tightens around the cloak of identity. When the sense of being-awareness is recognized to be still present but simply obscured, one can feel a loosening and relaxation, as though one no longer feels quite as separated from the immediacy of being.

John: True. When the recognition comes back to the fact of ever-present being, the focus on thoughts subsides, and there is the immediate recognition of the natural freedom inherent in being-awareness.

Q: Nonetheless, this experience that obscuration brings about, does appear to create all the suffering, the sense of identity in a separate self.

John: Well, you can refine the view here. It is more accurate to say that the sense of self generates a flow of self-centered thinking, which is synonymous with suffering. So the belief in a separate self is the root of the experience.

Q: When this clouding over occurs, clarity is not always quick in returning, and it is easy to be swept away into the story of me, other and all else.

John: Try not to fall into the trap of thinking the clarity comes and goes. It decidedly does not. Even when suffering thoughts appear, can you deny the presence of awareness? So, upon deeper looking, you can see that that clarity does not come and go. We were just looking in the wrong direction.

Q: Still, when this clouding over occurs, it is very frustrating! The frustration compounds this, because of the desire to have whatever is happening, including the frustration, be otherwise.

John: This is just more self-centered thinking. Just see clearly what is happening. The seeing is enough to snap the fixation on the thought and you return immediately to clarity. Or, more accurately, you discover you never actually left it.

Q: I can see that from this perspective there is no question of 'What to do?' simply because then, immediately, it becomes obvious that doing is a continuation of the story-line of 'me'. Even reading the books or websites that point to the reality of this being-awareness is more doing, albeit helpful in loosening up the grip of mind-stuff. However, reminders do continue to help in clearing this up, just like the wind continues to sweep the clouds away, letting the light that is continuously present shine. Clouding over and the questions do continue to be part of life, though less frequently. I am grateful for the reminders.

John: All of this sinks in and becomes clearer. Once you see that awareness is clear, bright and constant, you will lose the sensation that clarity comes and goes. When we feel that clarity comes and goes, we are still putting more attention on thoughts. When you see that the awareness is the essential factor, you put the focus on the awareness itself and see that thoughts just come and go in the steady light of presence-awareness. From the point of view of awareness there is no problem with the presence or absence of thoughts. In truth, even self-centered thoughts do not actually touch or obscure your real being. Look into this and verify it for yourself. Then you will not need any more reminders!

71

The 'One-Two' Punch

Question: In your previous e-mail you asked me to consider this: If you really want to ace this quickly and directly, look into this Question:'What is the root and cause of self-centered thinking?' If self-centered thinking has a root cause and you eradicate it, could there be any more effects?

I pondered this and here is what came up. Painful thoughts and feelings arise, such as anger, resentment, sadness, fear—so what? Who is suffering? Is there anyone here who is suffering or are there just thoughts and feelings arising? Right now there is awareness, and awareness is what I am.

Thoughts and feelings arise. There is no controller here that creates these thoughts and feelings or that can change them or avoid them. They come and they go. There is no one here who suffers (other than the body), but there is no person here who can suffer. There is awareness—and in this, anything can arise. The thought that I should not be having certain feelings implies that there is someone here who can control thoughts and feelings. Where is this controller?

Other thoughts like 'I should have a mystical experience of universal love and union' and so on are just beliefs that were picked up from reading books about spirituality and enlightenment. Any thought that I should or should not do, be or have is just another thought or belief arising in me. So what? I am awareness. I am not touched by any thought or belief. There is no one in control of thoughts and beliefs. They just arise in me. So what?

The thought or belief that there is someone (me) that is in control of thoughts and feelings and a 'me' who can suffer is the root cause of self-centered thinking. There is no one in control and there is no one here who can suffer. All I am sure of is that there is awareness. Everything else is speculation.

John: You are getting to the root of this. Self-centered thoughts imply a self at their center. But this self is actually not something that we have completely verified to be present. So what you find is that self-centered thoughts are founded on the belief that there is a substantial, separate and independent self. Furthermore, there is the subsequent belief that this is what we are. Those two beliefs form the foundation of the whole network of self-centered thoughts (suffering).

In fact, self-centered thinking is just an attempt by the mind to stabilize or give some sense of solidity to that imagined self-center. With the rise of the notion of a separate 'I' comes in separation, vulnerability, fear and so on. The mind, assuming the root cause to be real, attempts to fix or heal the split by providing identities for that 'I', in order to make it solid and secure. The mind also devises various stratagems to try to recover happiness and wholeness. All of these various concepts and beliefs are just variants of self-centered thinking. Eventually, you find that there is no lasting solution in the mind's attempts to find security, wholeness and fulfillment. The vast majority of so-called spiritual techniques and disciplines tend to exacerbate the problem, because they only address the effects and not the fundamental cause.

So the belief in the existence of a separate self and our identity with that is the root of the problem. But eventually you come round to asking if the limited self that we have been taking ourselves to be is real or even present. If it is real, then we should be able to find it. So where is it? What is it actually? The thrust of this aspect of the inquiry really gets down to trying to find, locate, identify or perceive anything that could answer to the description of a separate, independently existing self. All self-centered thinking assumes the existence of this entity (and our identity as that).

But if nothing of the sort can be located or found, then what becomes of all the attributes and identifications that are associated with it? For example, if the thought is 'I am no good' and we look and cannot find any 'I', then who is no good? If the thought is 'I am not enlightened' and there is no 'I', then who is not enlightened and so on? Who is afraid? Who is separate? Who has a problem? This inquiry becomes all the more powerful when it is coupled with the simultaneous pointing out of the undeniable presence of awareness and our identity with that. This is the 'one-two' punch that will completely dismantle any remaining doubts or questions. Under no circumstances can you doubt the fact of your being, which is present and brightly aware, nor can you doubt your identity with that. And that is certainly not a separate, limited entity.

You come to see that all suffering is based on a cause which, upon investigation, is found to be completely non-existent. Seeing this, all possible doubts and questions are undermined and cannot survive. Simultaneously, you come to see that you are inseparable from that natural state of presence-awareness, which is inherently free, whole and complete. Everything that you are seeking is fully present but was just overlooked due to innocent ignorance. Once the basics are pointed out, you can see this and verify it for yourself in immediate experience. As I always say, no time is needed, only clear seeing. From this position, all seeking comes to an end and what has been pointed out in the teachings of non-duality is very clear and certain, not as an idea, but as unshakeable direct experience. Nothing or no one can shake you from this understanding. It is the fact of your being, and you are that.

Q: Very well put. You can take me out of the oven now. I am done! It is all good!

72

Don't Refuse to Be What You Are

Question: We have not communicated previously. I have read Bob Adamson's book a few times and listened to his CDs. Certain things rang true for me. Then I found your site. The first thing I noticed was that your picture seems familiar. (Is this a resonance?) In reading several articles, I soon realized what is being pointed to. It is so obvious. As I read, it was so clear what I am. There was such a feeling of relaxation. I have been caught in the mind for all my life, just as I was supposed to be. Things are less clear now that I am away from the site, but I feel very confident that something has happened and that this will deepen. I look forward to getting back home and reading some more of the site. I would like to thank you for what you have written, even though you had no choice in the matter!

John: Nice to hear from you. I am happy to hear something clicked for you and brought you back to your own direct, simple and clear knowing. If the pointers seem to work, stay with them. As you resonate more and more directly with what is being pointed to, take note of what you recognize. Then forget the pointers and simply rest in and as that. There are many words used to point to it. But, simply put, it is your own natural presence or being. It is open, clear, brightly aware. Everything else appears in this space of knowing. It is so utterly lucid and simple that we overlooked it—till now!

The mind creates suffering when it imagines that we are separate from this. Then various thoughts and beliefs arise based on this fundamental mistaken assumption. From the position of clear awareness, you can now see this for what it is—mistaken ideas. These ideas appear right in the awareness itself. Seeing all this, the search is pretty much over because the two primary facets of ignorance are exposed, which are 1) not knowing what we are, and 2) imagining ourselves to be what we are not. Nisargadatta Maharaj summed up the remedy in the following pithy statement:

'Don't pretend to be what you are not—Don't refuse to be what you are'.

You are now in a position to see this for yourself.

Utterly Beyond Doubt

John: Thoughts, perceptions and feelings come and go, but you remain. What is the nature of that 'you' that you are? You are that right now. Understand this clearly and you will know what needs to be known. It is nothing that you can see, observe or grasp, because you are singular. How could you see, observe or grasp yourself—as something apart? And yet you are most tangibly present and aware. This is utterly beyond doubt.

What is this 'no thing' that is present and brightly aware? It is the most important fact of our experience, but how many of us have probed into this question to discover the answer? This sums up the entire approach. If you apply yourself to seeing this for yourself, you will have the understanding you are looking for—in no time.

Emptiness and Fullness

Question: I found your article 'Utterly Beyond Doubt' very, very mind blocking. Yes, thoughts, perceptions and feelings come and go. Yesterday's thoughts, hopes and fears were different from today's. But to whom or to what do these thoughts appear? Who sees them? Who knows them? The answer that comes to mind is 'me'. All these happen to me. But if this me logically is different from these thoughts and feelings, then what is this 'me'? I cannot find it. I cannot locate it. And, finally, who asks these questions? Of course something is not going too well with these syllogisms! But I write them because they came immediately after reading the article. Thank you for your words which caused these urgent questions.

John: What you find is that you are undoubtedly present and aware. This is clear and cannot be questioned. You are that which observes and therefore transcends all thoughts, feelings and sensations—in short, everything objective. Viewing from the perspective of the senses or mind, what you are is not find-able. It is 'no thing'. It is an absence, an emptiness. There is simply nothing you can point out or grasp hold of as yourself.

But this emptiness that you are is present, clear, vivid, luminous and alive. It is that open space of presence-awareness. Some have called it 'cognizing emptiness'. That is the constant, timeless presence in which all appearances rise and set. It is the ground of being which all things come forth from and into which they resolve. Being the ground of everything, it is full and complete. What you are is emptiness and fullness, absence and presence.

In your true nature, the dream of separation has never occurred. Realizing what you are, the belief in being a separate person, which was the cause of all of our suffering, is exposed and uprooted conclusively and decisively. The questioner and his questions vanish. What remains is clarity, what I call the natural state.

75

Abide As the Peace That Is Your Real Nature

Question: Thanks for your help. The best way to describe my daily experience is to say that there is a steady sense of peace. Life feels very simple and easy.

You know, it was two weeks ago that I said I would like to 'nail this thing down in two weeks'. I feel pretty confident that it is nailed down. It seems that the real key was seeing and knowing that there is no person or controller here. Now I see that everything is happening, but to no one. Before, there was a sense that everything was happening to me, and that I had to take action to fix whatever I did not like and to hold onto everything that I did like. Now I see there is no one here.

There has been no suffering. I see there is no one here who can suffer. Distressing thoughts rarely arise and when they do, there is a sense that they are empty and meaningless. They have no target to hit and they fall to the ground. Before, one distressing thought could lead to hours of mental churning and anguish. Now, thoughts come and go like leaves blowing in the wind. Where did they come from? Where are they going? Who cares?

It is clear that there is no doer here in me. I also see that there is no doer in anyone else. Everything is happening, but no one is doing anything. It is all quite a mystery. Seeing that there is no one here (or there), I notice a natural sense of compassion arising. Maybe this is the love we refer to as our natural state. It is not an egoic love but a general sense of peace and compassion. There is not a 'me' who loves a 'you', but just this peaceful compassion.

I do not feel that I have gained anything. It seems more that I have lost the sense of 'me' that was disturbing the peace that was already here. Maybe I did gain the understanding that there is no 'me' here and there is no 'you' there. I do not know. But I do know there is peace. Well, thanks for your help, John, and I will stay in touch.

John: Thanks for the note. What you are saying strikes me as a simple and clear statement of your direct experience. You say 'I do not feel that I have gained anything. It seems more that I have lost the sense of 'me' that was disturbing the peace that was already here'. This is excellent and is exactly what is being pointed out. To live outside of the reference to a 'me' leaves you in a direct experience of peace. Just abide there. You will find that this is just the natural state of presence and clarity that is always with you.

Everyone is searching for peace and contentment. Now you see the source of peace (your own true nature) and have seen through what seemed to obstruct it (the apparent 'me', which drove the network of suffering and doubt). The residual belief in a 'me' and habitual thoughts based on that may appear in thought and memory due to habit, but the core driver, which is the belief in their reality, has been exposed. You will never be able to buy back into that framework again. If there is any doubt about whether there is a separate 'me' or not, simply look in your direct experience and see if you can find yourself as being anything apart from the simple fact of presence-awareness. The recognition dawns and then settles into certainty that the separate self has never, ever existed. All there is is that presence of awareness, clarity, the natural state—whatever you want to call it. That is simply what you are. You know this now. Abide in and as the peace that is your real nature.

What You Are Is Already Present

Question: There seems to be a very good understanding of what is being pointed at. When thought is paused for a moment, I remain (aware, alive and conscious). But, there is no peace or contentment that I read so much about. Is it just thoughts and feelings arising that seem to constantly hide the clarity and peace. I am not looking for fireworks, but some definite peace would be nice! Maybe I have too many expectations? The most important thing seems to just be and let this understanding do its job and maybe peace and clarity will be self evident?

John: Just remember that what you are (the simple fact of being and awareness) is also peace. Whenever the mind is not focused on self-centered thoughts, peace is automatically there. The simplest example is deep sleep. Our attention has been so long focused on the objects of perception that when awareness is pointed out, it seems subtle and almost intangible. If you look for fireworks and grand experiences, you will overlook the simplicity of your ever-present true nature. Give it a chance to reveal itself.

Continue to turn away from the doubts and riddles created in thought and probe into the presence-awareness itself. That is where the treasure lies. Your true nature is not an experience or future event. If you hold onto that belief, you will overlook the simplicity of what is being pointed to. Remember, what you are looking for is something already present. There are some recent postings on my website of people sharing their own experiences of understanding. You may want to refer to those articles to see how this has unfolded for others, like you, who are looking into this.

Thoughts Do Not Stick to You

Question: I just thought I would touch base with you to give you a 'progress report'. I have just been letting the vision reveal its depths as I continue to return to the basics and be astounded by the effortless wonder of the 'I'-less state. The ongoing realization that who I am is not all those limited ideas I had about myself is really helping me deal with my work and personal life much more naturally. Seeing infinite happiness, peace and freedom as the incontrovertible essence of who I am, no matter what seems to be happening at the relative level, allows life to take care of itself quite nicely without the need for a 'me' to direct it. I still occasionally notice the old traces of the seeking mind trying to re-assert themselves. But with a little self-questioning, the delusion is almost just as quickly dissolved. So again, I cannot thank you enough for helping me to realize I have been seeing it all along!

John: Thanks for the note. Everything you are saying sounds excellent. With the basics now under your belt, things settle in. As you say, there may be some old reactions and habits coming through, but they are easily seen and recognized for what they are—thought patterns arising in the clear awareness that you are. Clouds do not stick to or bother the sky, and thoughts do not stick to you. The best meditation is just to do nothing! As thoughts and experiences come, so they go, leaving you ever free and untouched. I am happy that this understanding has dawned for you. Good news.

Q: (A poem):

> No-time.
> No-thing.
> Thought-clouds move silently
> across the sky.
> No one there
> to perceive them.

Thanks, John, for keeping the light burning!

78

Take Care of the Basics

Question: In general I feel somewhat more detached from the manifestation. Things do not seem to be bothering me to the extent that they usually do. There is something else on top of all this, and that is that, once in a while, I step back and say that all of this is just appearing. Sometimes I take it to be significant that I am having these insights, but then I realize that in a broader sense I am seeing this happen from a more basic viewpoint. Something in me is silent. There is just a watching and a knowing that the whole thing is just part of the play. And then I wonder—so what must be beyond this realization? If I see (and I am not saying that I do) that I am not a person, that everyone else is not a person, but everything is that, as a vibration of energy at the core level, then what is next?

John: It is the mind (usual suspect!) asking 'What is beyond?' and so on. As a practical matter, I would say take care of the basics—the primacy of awareness and the absence of separation. Marinate in that a bit. Then see if there are even any questions left. I will suggest that all questions and doubts are just generated in thought, based on a subtle reference to an imagined entity. It is interesting to note how—for a period of time—we still reference the mind and the doubts as our yardstick for what is important. We are looking for some subtle shift, state or confirmation. But I ask, what is wrong with awareness right now? And are you separate from that? In awareness, all the normal thoughts and sensations go on just fine, so there is no need to look for some amazing shift. There is no amazing shift needed. Even if one happens, it will soon disappear anyway, for whatever comes, goes. Continue to emphasize awareness and your identity with that. Let any appearances be as they are. Rest in and as your true nature and see what comes up and is revealed. What is awareness, what does it feel like, what is it like to sense and know one's identity with that? Knowing this, then what remains of one's assumed identity as a person or separate entity?

Question: Somehow I think I would be enjoying this more if I had no work to do. The procrastination is at an all time high!

John: So, tell me who is beating your heart, making the sun shine, making the wind blow? Is that a 'you'? Are you doing any of those things? So this work that you are talking about, who is doing that? The work is not the problem! There is really no one present to either do it or not do it. What is strenuous and tiring is hanging onto the belief in the existence of a self-center. As usual, we look away from the real cause and misidentify the problem as 'out there'. Who is this 'I' that is doing or not doing work? Is there any such thing?

79

Awareness is a Fact, Not a Future Experience

Question: I have written to you once before to thank you for your marvelous writings. Your particular approach really makes sense to me. I do not rely on books much anymore, but the full understanding (or what I have experienced of it) apparently does not stay for long.

John: But through any of this, can you say that your being departed or did not stay for long? By definition, states and experiences come and go. If we have a subtle expectation that the answer lies there, we continue to believe that we are missing something. Keep things very simple. The answer is the fact of your own present being and awareness. That is what is being pointed to. That is your real nature, who you truly are. So, through all the ups and downs of experience, does this leave you?

Q: The times when I know that there is nothing to achieve, that this moment is all there is, that the clear looking at 'what is' is all there is—this aware state only occurs periodically.

John: But awareness does not occur periodically. It is the unchanging and constant background of all experience. It is a simple fact, not a future experience to wait for.

Q: After a time, I slip back into the mind-world of problems and things that have to be solved and fixed.

John: You must get very clear on what is happening. I have covered the 'mechanics' of the origin of suffering in previous writings. If you understand this, you will have a very clear view of what is happening when we apparently lose the recognition of our true nature. Once you understand the basics of how this works, you will easily reclaim the natural state of freedom from thoughts.

Q: I am so tired of the cycle, but apparently not tired enough!

John: Well, there is still a referencing of the belief in a separate one who can get something or lose it!

Q: Perhaps I will have the chance to speak with you at some point. I know that I do not have to travel anywhere to be what I am, but I am apparently still wandering around the store, lost and attached to the pretty objects! I can continue to be patient, knowing that I cannot actually do anything, but do I have to be?

John: Continue to review the pointers in my book and on my website. You will find several recent articles by people who have seen this themselves. It may be helpful to read about how the understanding has unfolded for them. If they can see the basics, so can you!

80

Have You Ever Left Presence?

Question: Thanks again so much for taking time to talk with me. It was so useful and illuminating. Thank you for being so patient. Believe me, I appreciate how many different ways you said the same thing. It has been said that when the student is truly ready the right teacher shows up. These may be 'hocus pocus' words, I know, but then again! I am grateful for your friendship and counsel.

John: Keep up the looking and inquiring until you are sure you see the basics clearly for yourself. You are what you are seeking. Be sure of that. Look at all questions and doubts in the light of this. Remember, all suffering, doubts and questions hang on a tacit referencing to an imagined self-center. Inquire into this until you are sure that there is no such thing. That leaves you with a clear and unwavering recognition of your true nature as presence-awareness or whatever other term you prefer! Even now, you are nothing other than this. Thought, emotions and perceptions do not touch this. They are all only expressions of this and, ultimately, are one with it (you).

Q: The understanding is simple and clear, but it is still in the mind, for I still have a sense of 'in here' and 'out there'. The sense that this dream includes me, not as the dreamer but the dreamed, all one in and on awareness is not yet apperceived, as Nisargadatta Maharaj might say. I try to just allow this, the percolation. I know well that the I in here is not. It is just mind in the way. So how to let mind do its thing and get a sense of what is real beyond it and all else? I have turned around and am looking inward. All sense of finding anything out there is gone. It will be here that my true nature is uncovered, period. That in itself is liberating.

You wrote 'You are what you are seeking. Be sure of that. Look at all questions and doubts in the light of this'. This line opened up to me when I re-read it today. If I am what I am seeking—and I am sure of that—then no amount or clever kind of mind seeking will do anything but keep me on the rat wheel. So why not rest in being that and 'in the light of this' just be. What will open up will open up no sooner, no later.

In Ashtanga yoga the mantra is 'practice and all is forthcoming'. The mind, it seems, is a muscle with great strength and ever so subtle dexterity. But if it is not flexed and nuanced it will wither, so it seems to me. When you were with Bob Adamson, how did it change for you?

John: Stay with your identity as presence-awareness. This is the essential point. Know for certain that nothing gets in the way of this. The only thing that appears to do so is thoughts, particularly thoughts based on the idea that you are a limited, separate and problematic person.

Look straight at this and see how all the suffering is various forms of self-centered thinking—worries, doubts, cares, problems, identifications of the apparent limited, defective self. See the workings of this clearly—like the lines on the palm of your hand. Realize that all the self-centered thoughts hang on the subtle belief in the person, the small self. If that is questioned and found to be false or absent, the root cause of suffering—all suffering—is pulled out. See all this for yourself. See if you can find any such thing as an abiding, separate entity. This will undercut the self-centered thoughts or tendencies. And throughout all this, have you ever left presence? Has the fact of awareness and your identity with it been lost?

At this point, you do not need any more basic pointers. The key is to apply the basic understanding to your own experience. If any questions or doubts arise, dismantle them in the light of the basic pointers. Come back to the doubtless fact of being.

You asked: 'When you were with Bob Adamson, how did it change for you?' I can talk about my experience to offer some encouragement, but now you are in the test tube! This is your story, not mine! I will take the high road here and just say that this question arises in thought. The mind is interested in finding an answer. Just see that this question is appearing right in clear, present, open awareness. That is the answer. When you try to find out what someone else meant or what their experience is or was, you move away from the direct recognition of your own present freedom. The recognition of your nature as awareness is the key. Turning to the mind for answers and to learn what is true about what we are is where we went wrong way back when. Now you can clear that up once and for all.

81

Refuse to Believe False Concepts

Question: Thank you for your e-mail. I have been reading the articles on your website. The way things are here now is as follows. There is awareness every time it is noticed. It seems constant and changeless. There is no separate me. That is mostly a thought arising. The mind (or rather thoughts) appears to come relentlessly and constantly. When there is a moment of no thought, I remain aware and conscious and alive. This state seems to be calmer and quieter (very brief moments). So, if there is no separate me, then even by default, there is no he, she or you. So, all people are just appearances in consciousness. However, there is no felt sense of oneness or whatever. There is still a very strong identification with the body-mind. The forgetting of my real nature happens over and over again. But the remembering also seems to happen (occasionally) that I am not body or mind. I am the awareness that knows and is aware of body and mind.

John: There is no need to wait for an event, experience, feeling of oneness and so on. That is looking to the appearance or to the mind for an answer, which is bound to fail. There is nothing wrong with the arising of thoughts. A state of no thoughts is not more preferable or closer to the imagined state you are seeking. And you cannot remember or forget your true being of awareness. Remembering and forgetting are just mind states arising and setting in presence-awareness. It is the focus on these false concepts that can hang you up. Presence-awareness is open, clear and available. So do not turn away from this and give credence to these subtle beliefs.

When you refuse to believe these false concepts, your identity with presence-awareness will stand out in all clarity. It is there even now, but you are giving more emphasis to the concepts than the truth of who you are.

Remember, this is not about bringing in a new state. It is really a dismantling of all false beliefs that kept us from noticing the ever-present obvious. Constantly and at all times you shine as that. It is not a matter of forgetting or remembering. It is a fact. Thoroughly question all ideas and beliefs to the contrary.

82

All Problems and Doubts Are for a Phantom

Question: I have been spending a lot of time going back to the basics. It is feeling really comfortable. I read the e-mail about the person who gave himself a couple of weeks to get this and it resonated with me. As we have discussed before, it is easy to see that you are awareness, and that has been great. It is harder to dis-identify with the conceptual 'I'. You said in one of your posts that thoughts were just 'whirling energy' and there was no 'I' in the center of thought.

I was trying to do a process of elimination. Where is the 'I'? What possibilities are there for an 'I' to exist? So when there is an apparent 'I' in the center of your thoughts (during suffering, self-centered thinking) then that is basically all there can be of an 'I'. That is it. That is the only 'I' that is possible—an illusory concept that makes a temporary appearance in this whirling energy and then is gone. (Of course it can be repeated enough in thought to elicit emotion and suffering.) The body is an object in awareness, so there is no 'I' there. The only place you could possibly find an 'I' is in thought, which is also an appearance. Am I on track here? There sure is not much here for an 'I' to hang onto, is there? I have had several really good days with this. Maybe it is starting to unravel a little.

John: You are definitely on track with this. If you have a good look and cannot find any substantial 'I' in the picture, then who or what does all the self-centered thinking apply to? Nothing! All the doubts, problems, questions, seeking and so on are for a phantom that does not exist. Certainly they do not pertain to you, because you are already that ever-free awareness that is what all the teachings are pointing to.

Presence-awareness remains clear, open, rock solid and beyond doubt. And have you ever been separate from that? If you are in doubt—then check it out! Once you begin to question the imagined self-center and discover it is a fiction, the 'whole shit house goes up in flames' to quote a line from Jim Morrison of the Doors.

Q: I am definitely ready for the 'shit house' to go up in flames. What you are saying has been interesting, and I want to sit with it and follow up in a few days. One of the other things you said that really resonated was 'There is awareness. There are a handful of thoughts, perceptions, and feelings arising in the moment—but that is all. All else is imagination, that is, not really present except as a concept'. That is clearly seen of late. Just clear as a bell, easy to notice. The conceptual 'I' is a little looser in the saddle at the moment.

John: Well, I would suggest that you shoot that bad boy right out of the saddle. Assuming you can find him!

Q: Ha! Yep, the lil' devil 'I' may be slippin' off his horse soon. Two weeks? Nah! One at the most.

John: Get the 'I' clearly in your sights, then we can talk about how long. I am still having trouble finding him!

Q: OK. The important thing is that it is clear what I am noticing and how to get back to it.

John: Yes, notice that the idea of being something separate and apart from present awareness cannot be verified on direct evidence. This is the trumpet blast that brings the walls of Jericho tumbling down.

Q: This is powerful stuff. If you are never separate and apart from present awareness, then there can never be, for example, the person who believes they are rejected and unloved. That is, you can never be your story. If present awareness includes interaction with another person, it includes what present awareness always includes, a handful of thoughts and sensations arising in the background of clear awareness. Only the conceptual 'I', separate and apart, can be unloved, rejected in the past or fear rejection in the future. Awareness by its very nature always stands clear of the story.

John: … and the walls come a-tumblin' down!

Form and Emptiness are Just Concepts

Question: I have settled into presence-awareness per your advice, which was the soundest I received. Thoughts arise out of the open space, which remains stable amid all their change Despite that, the mind raises a question, mainly because of my Zen Buddhist background. One of Zen's central tenets is couched by the Heart Sutra—*'Form is emptiness and emptiness, form. Emptiness is not other than form; form is not other than emptiness'*. This would seem to imply that neither is prior. Thoughts arise out of the open space and the open space arises from thoughts.

John: Just see that when you try to figure out the various teachings in the mind, you move away from the immediate clarity that you are. Advaita and Buddhism are undoubtedly saying the same thing. They are just different formulations of words. As such they are bound to be different in expression. Very few, if any, ever came to clarity by studying philosophy, even Buddhism or Advaita Vedanta. That is a simple fact. Such study tends to emphasize thought and takes you away from the simple and obvious. The more you think about it the farther away it gets. Simply drop thought and notice immediate, bright, vivid, open, spacious, non-conceptual, non-objective presence-awareness. It is utterly empty, yet utterly full.

Pure awareness is emptiness. Everything arises in and upon this cognizing emptiness. What appears has no independent existence and is non-separate from emptiness. There is only one thing, not two. To talk about form and emptiness is still a concession to ignorance and is not the deepest view. It is still in the realm of duality—emptiness and form. Non-duality means not two. All objects are reducible to thought. When you look at thought closely it is only a vibration or movement with no substance. Its content (that is, the material from which it is made) is just awareness. So, all that exists ultimately is awareness. That is utterly non-objective, empty, space-like and void of any characteristics. From the point of view of the mind and senses it is nothing. Yet it is certainly not inert or a void of nothingness. It is your true nature, upstream of thought.

Form and emptiness are just concepts. Drop them as irrelevant. Abide as the true nature that you have always been since before time ever was. You wrote: 'Thoughts arise out of the open space and the open space arises from thoughts'. This is problematic and I feel is not clear. Sure, thoughts arise from awareness, but does awareness arise from thought? The latter is dubious. Thoughts are inert, fleeting insubstantial, with no real sentience or existence. Ultimately, in essence, they are awareness. But at the level of thought, they certainly do not generate or create awareness. You are aware of thought. Thought may create the concept of 'you' (as a mental representation), but it certainly does not create your fundamental nature, which is utterly beyond the reach of thought.

You need to be careful of the level from which you are speaking. Many seekers lack a deep and penetrating realization of emptiness because often the looking is done at an intellectual level. This is just food for non-thought!

Q: Wise words. Thanks. Starting out as a novice, the terms, 'awareness', 'presence', 'form', 'emptiness', carried a certain provenance. They are each appropriately descriptive, but for a novice I found the best was 'is-ness'. It offered turf relatively unstaked by any camp. We are pure subjectivity, all of us. Open and spacious is-ness cannot be doubted. You may recall that I said I would settle into the question. While waiting to hear from you, the issue was resolved by remembering my use of the word 'is-ness' and ultimately by just letting go of all the terms. Your reply nonetheless gave a needed nudge.

You are right, little pockets of ignorance remain, as shown by this e-mail. That is why somebody like you is a blessing. It was good to hear from you. Your support and kindness have been priceless.

John: Your writings and communication show that the understanding is taking solid root. Yes, a few odds and ends may arise, a few doubts and questions here and there. Why not? The conditioned thoughts have been cultivated and believed in for years. But that is not a problem. The innate intelligence comes in as needed and exposes the false assumptions and ideas. At this point, you can settle for nothing less than the complete freedom that you already know is your natural state. Good to hear from you and keep in touch.

84

Everything Seems So Simple Now

Question: Thank you for your guidance and support. I really appreciate it. In a sense nothing has changed in my life, yet everything has changed. I feel that all the words and concepts we have been talking about and reading about for so many years have become my daily living experience. Everything seems so simple now. All of the great teachings that have been written in thousands of pages in hundreds of books have all come down to just this! This simplicity of being. This is it!

Looking back at all the years of searching and suffering I cannot imagine how I could possibly have missed this. I have read it all a thousand times. I understood it intellectually all so well, but the suffering continued. The simplicity of this is absolutely mind-boggling. Life continues as it always has, but there is this new perspective that is not really new, yet it is completely new because there is no suffering.

All I can say is thank you for pointing me in the right direction and showing me how simple this is, simple yet profound. I am very thankful that you are doing what you are doing and sharing your experience with this. I really think that it is possible that I could have spent twenty more years chasing my own tail had you not been here to snap me out of it. Thank you.

I feel moved to share this with anyone who has an interest. I know what a great impact your guidance has had on my life and if this can be shared with others I will feel blessed to help.

John: It is always great to see when the bug takes hold! Your seeing of this is solid. Once the basics are seen, there is a natural desire to share the good news. Just let it flow in whatever way it comes up. The expression develops and you find ways to share that work for you and those you meet. The more you share it, the more potent it gets.

The Good News

Question: I just wanted to thank you for being so clear and helping me to cross over with your book 'Awakening to the The Natural State'. I have been waiting for a book precisely like yours but was beginning to think it was just wishful thinking. I have been studying contemporary non-dual literature for about the past five years and am glad to find out it has always been this way. I could not have seen it without your help. I am from Indiana and around this neck of the woods everything is so fundamentally Christian. It has been a long time coming. Thanks for your clear insight.

John: I am glad to have provided a few pointers back to your ever-present and clear state of presence-awareness. Once Bob Adamson pointed this out to me, I thought the least I could do was to pass along the good news. I enjoyed your e-mail. Stay in touch if you like, if anything comes up to share.

Recognize Awareness Non-Conceptually

Question: There is the feeling for me that there is still something else. I wonder if it is an intuitive feeling or just the mind playing itself out with another expectation? Yes, I understand that there is awareness and all else appears in that. The question is about omnipresence. I am still perceiving from a point of perception, as if I am behind these eyes. Is that the same for you or do you experience from everywhere and nowhere?

I was looking at the question 'Who am I?' some months ago. I watched the mind looking for and grabbing onto concept after concept. In the end, it was clear that 'I' was the one that was always aware of the concept. It gave the feeling that I was always behind, a sense of omnipresence, not seeing from a fixed point. So do you understand that you are omnipresent or is there the direct experience of it?

John: Omnipresence is a concept. Do not get too hung up on it. Look straight at awareness itself. Where does it start? Where does it end? Does it have any borders or edges? Is it lodged behind the eyes or anywhere else? Thoughts, perceptions, eyes and so on are all limited and bounded in space, time and location. But can you say the same about the fact of awareness? And what is your relationship with awareness? Are you separate from awareness? Do not think about awareness. Recognize it non-conceptually in direct seeing. Knowing your real nature has little to do with thinking about it!

You Are Already Complete

Question: Well, it has been twelve days since our phone conversation.

John: Yet has there been any change in your identity as ever-present awareness? Remember that time is just a concept fabricated in thought and does not apply to your real nature.

Q: I felt a powerful shift and, I think, completion.

John: Question this and knock the concept out. There is no need for completion or a shift. You are already complete. It is the recognition of what is already totally clear and present in you. That has always been there. Shifts and completions are in terms of the mind that is in time and measurement. I understand where you are coming from, but it is good to expose those ideas fully and to be precise and emphatic.

Q: However, there has certainly not been a steady resting in awareness.

John: For whom? Who is there who needs to rest? Are you something apart from awareness? Awareness is awareness, and that is what you are. There is no entity present who can rest or not rest.

Q: There have been instances, as you reported in your own experience, where the thought arose that I had lost it.

John: But that is only a thought arising in the ever-present clarity that you are. It is a false idea based on a misunder-standing of what is being pointed to. How can you lose your own aware presence, when even the thought 'I lost it' is arising right in that very same awareness? See this clearly and the feeling of getting it and losing it is over for good—right now.

Q: It is very difficult—perhaps impossible—to assess all this, as that would imply an object (myself) which I have seen is fictional. There is awareness always, even when I still identify with a thought out of habit.

John: Yes, but who is that 'I' that identifies with thought? What are you talking about actually?

Q: Yes, I can see that my last statement cannot be real either because there is no 'me' to identify. It is just wordplay again!

John: Yes. You see it!

Q: There seems to be a real absence of seeking now, although there is a definite support in the reminders from your writings.

John: They just bring you back to what you have seen and now know for yourself. As this settles in you will not need reminders anymore.

Q: Well, that is the latest summary of things. It would be fun to visit you in Santa Cruz, but it seems unnecessary. The realization feels core to my existence, confirmed by our conversation.

John: Strictly speaking meeting in person is not necessary because what is being realized is right within you. How could being here enhance that in any way? But if you are in the area or have the chance to visit, it would be nice to meet. All sounds good. Stay in touch as the spirit moves.

88

You Are the One That Is Awake, No One Else

Question: You say suffering arises from thought only. So if someone ran up and plunged a knife into your chest you would not suffer? I am not talking about physical pain here. If you could endure that and no thoughts came up, I guess there would be no suffering. This does not make sense to me. If pure awareness is it, it seems to be an ignorant state. There is still a separation between that and the creation of all that we perceive. If we are in the natural state, how did we come up with the idea of humans, bugs, fish and so on. I do not understand that someone can claim to be awake and still perceive all this.

What does this natural state reveal? Does it grow in depth? As far as I can see, there seems to be a big difference between various people who claim to be awake. Of course that assumes all who say they are awake really are. Does this understanding change your character or personality? If you see the person as simply thoughts, an illusory dream, then what? What if you were abusive, cruel or even criminal before? Does that change?

If there is no doer, then awakening is just another happening. So if I am not lucky, it is not going to happen to me, right? By the looks of things, it is not going to happen here, unfortunately.

John: I do not believe in so-called awake people. You exist and you are aware. You are not a body, mind, person or anything else. You are simply that undeniable presence of awareness that is with you right now. You are the one that is awake, no one else! All the questions and doubts are imagined in thought and do not touch who you are. Seeing this is all that is being pointed to. If you are having a hard time with the basic teachings of non-duality, check out some of standard sources of non-dual teachings. The writings of 'Sailor' Bob Adamson are good. I have links to other sources listed on my website. All the questions you are dealing with have been covered in this material.

You suffer because you do not clearly know who you are. Knowing who you are ends the seeking, questions, doubts and suffering. Of course the body feels sensations, including pain. There is nothing wrong with that.

As I said, as far as I am concerned there are no awake people. You are awareness itself. That is all you really need to know.

Q: Yes, I have read everything on your site, 'Sailor' Bob's site, John Greven's site and on and on. I have some books on Ramana Maharshi. I have read some on-line material about Nisargadatta Maharaj. I have a whole wall of books! OK. So I am awareness itself. Well, until I see it and it informs me of what you know, why don't you just answer my questions? I am getting old, and it looks like it is not going to be in the destiny of this body-mind to see it!

John: Stop and ask yourself if you are present and aware. If you answer yes, then stop again. That is what is being pointed to. Are there any doubts about the fact of your own being? Any questions, problems or doubts that come up are generated in thought based on the subtle belief that you are something apart from this clear, effortless and natural presence-awareness. Once that belief is questioned and discarded, all the problems are undercut. Your own awareness is undoubtedly present. It is nothing you need to get because you already are what you are seeking. If this is not clear, have another look.

So the body is old. It is an object in awareness. How old is awareness? Are you the body or are you that which is aware of the body? This is all so simple that we overlook what is being pointed out. Past a point, reading just takes you in the wrong direction. I do not feel obliged to answer each and every question because they all turn out to be bogus. They are all based on a fundamental misunderstanding. The questions are not answered—they are discarded as being beside the point. The very fact of your presence, your own awareness, is the answer you are seeking. Let this sink in. The material on my website and in my book says everything I could possibly say in words. In fact, it is far more than is needed or necessary to realize what is being pointed to. Of course, it is up to you to have a look and verify the pointers for yourself. Neither I nor anyone else can do this for you.

Bring this back to fundamentals. Who is reading these words right now? What is the doubtless sense of presence-awareness in you that is registering everything in your experience? Look into that, for that is where the true answer lies. All other questions can wait. In fact, when you understand what you are, the other questions do not even need to be answered.

89

Effortless Presence-Awareness Is What You Are

Question: Your message has been driven home here. It is effortless joy, clarity and love, stemming from seeing, in direct experience, what I thought I was and what I am. The person is not there—so clear. It is not there! The cognizing-emptiness is there. And experience arising and subsiding in it. It is so unexpected to come across your teaching like this and such a revelation to occur in such a simple, clear and undeniable manner.

The fear, based on memory, of losing this is lurking nearby, as well as the desire to ask you those old questions about how to get it once and for good, not to mention an infinite network of wrong assumptions and habits. All of this is so tiring!

It boils down to resting in this recognition, doesn't it? That is all. Well, enough of words for now.

John: Just see that this effortless presence-awareness is what you are. No thought or experience can shake you from it. It is such a clear and simple fact, but it is completely outside of the realm of thought, so we overlooked it. But that has now changed. All the habits and doubts get undercut when you see this, because they were all driven by a belief that you were separate and apart from reality. It all spun out from a simple misunderstanding. Once that is corrected, everything falls into place naturally. If something needs to be looked at or seen, that will come up. Still, the fundamental fact of your true nature is now apparent to you. Everything else is just a concept that has no power to alter this. The individual that was generating the doubts and fears is discovered to be absent. You shine as the doubtless presence of awareness that is inherently free and complete from the beginning. It is wonderful that you see this now.

90

You Are Never Separate From This

Question: Can it be said that we are pure awareness and then when the mind comes in, it is the arising of the conceptual 'I'?

John: You could say that. Also see that the arising of thoughts does not really create any real separate 'I. It is just a movement of energy, a vibration in awareness. Nothing is really happening in the ultimate sense. In the thinking, the mind can create an imaginary reference point, a seeming sense of 'I'. But it is only a thought, a notion. There is really nothing of the sort present.

Q: I could see that there was only awareness and then as thoughts start coming in there was an understanding that it was the conceptual 'I' beginning to make its appearance.

John: Yes, although thoughts can play through. There is no one to whom they refer or who can claim them. I tend to view it as thoughts come in and then create the notion of separation. Although you could also make the case that separation is imagined and thoughts are born from that. When you look straight at awareness, there are no thoughts or separation in it at all.

Q: Before thought arose, there was no 'I'.

John: Yes, this is true. 'I' is created in thinking. It is a thought. Even the differentiation between thought and no-thought is also a thought! You are presence-awareness. This is doubtless. Everything that seems to appear cannot be separated from that. It has no real substance or existence apart from you, and so it must be, in the final analysis, what you are.

Q: In the past, there was this effort to differentiate 'practical' thought from 'self-centered' thought, but if I lump all thought as 'mind' or 'I' it seems to clear things up.

John: The presence or absence of thoughts is not a problem. The main thing to notice is that there never has been any actual thing as a separate 'I', except as an imagined notion. The mind, if you perceive it, is just a ripple in the ever-present, bright and clear awareness that you are. Seeing this, you are basically cooked. There is just nothing to do with it. Right from the beginning that is what you are. There is no need for revelations or dropping pennies. Right here, right now can you deny the fact of present awareness and your identity with that? I would say you are about fully baked, wouldn't you?

Q: Yes, I think so. Just about. There may be a few bubbles left to pop, a little finishing off. It was very clear this morning that everything is just happening. There is no cook in the kitchen, so to speak. There is no doubt that this is all much clearer than has been the case when I got excited about it all a few times before. I do not think there will be a lot more identification with thought. But, then, I have been there before, so I do not want to get too excited yet. I see what I am. And I see what I am not. So, as you are so fond of saying, I will let this 'resonate' a bit and see what comes out of the oven. Yes?

John: Any question or doubt would be arising right in this doubtless clarity that you now see and that you are. And who is there who would get it or not, have a doubt, get excited or not and so on? These are all interesting attributes of a phantom character that we still have not been available to find. When we look, all there is—everywhere and at all times—is rock-solid and certain presence-awareness. You can never find yourself as something separate and apart from this.

91

Presence Is Not Difficult to Sustain

Question: I never realized how incredibly difficult it is to sustain presence.

John: Presence is not difficult to sustain. It is just an ongoing fact. No effort is required or necessary.

Q: What a hilarious cosmic joke. The thing that is the simplest and the purest (remaining present) is utterly impossible for the mind. It is so funny. What a wonderful exercise in recognizing the utter fallibility and futility of the mind. Presence-awareness is so not about the mind!

John: Very true. It is good that you see this.

Q: While I cannot say that seeing this has obliterated the cobwebs in an overt way, it has sure made me laugh. The mind is such silliness. That it has such an apparent stronghold is sheer lunacy. And yet, I see clearly that if one were capable of being truly, wholly present even for an instant, the mind would simply die through recognizing its own transparency.

John: If? Capable? For an instant? What are you right now, except totally obvious presence-awareness? Do not turn this into a state, an event, a moment of seeing. Right here, right now that which you are is fully present and clear. Let the old ideas about getting something, waiting for a future time and setting up preconditions utterly fall away.

Q: Your book had an interesting effect on me. The words

ultimately disappeared. Their meaning disappeared. The pointers disappeared. All there was, was the overall energy. There was just vast, all encompassing, definitive energy, non-tangible, yet undeniable. Lucky me!

John: Yes, but instead of saying 'all there was', I would say 'all there is'. Lucky, indeed! The 'you' is utterly lost in the seeing that you are non-different from presence-awareness. Ramana Maharshi said, 'Your greatest glory lies where you cease to exist'.—that is, as a separate entity apart from that.

92

Did You Ever Really Have a Problem?

Question: When reading your book, I began to find it challenging not to compare myself (my level of understanding or degree of progress) with some of the people who wrote to you who were clearly 'getting it'. It was as if some of them were waking up right there on the page. I was beginning to feel that even though I have been immersed in these teachings for 17 years that I still did not really have a clue. You previously wrote to me and said:

> '*Presence is not difficult to sustain. It is just an ongoing fact. No effort required or necessary. What are you right now, except totally obvious presence-awareness? Do not turn this into a state, an event, a moment of seeing. Right here, right now that which you are is fully present and clear. Let the old ideas about getting something, waiting for a future time and setting up preconditions utterly fall away! The 'you' is utterly lost in the seeing that you are non-different from presence-awareness'.*

This was so clear and admittedly a bit painful to hear. Of course I know all of these things to be so. I have read these words hundreds of times over the years, and have even said them to others. I feel so utterly frustrated sometimes because it is simply absurd that I have not truly seen this. It is simple, simple, simple and as unconscious as breathing. I know this to the core. There is nothing stopping me from waking up from the dream right now—absolutely nothing! All there is and can only be is presence. I have absolutely no doubts about this. It is the dream that befuddles me. It is the mind's fascination and seeming identification with the dream that completely shocks me. That 'still voice' inside of me is the wellspring. It is my nourishment. I am totally confident about that and totally at peace. I honestly do not get what the point is of there even needing to seemingly be a dream. What is it there for, other than to possibly serve as the relevant contrast, the reflection of something other, in order for presence to be recognized?

John: It gets very simple once you see that your true nature is already present. In fact, you already know this so it does not need to be pointed out. It is the simple fact of presence, which is evident and beyond doubt at all times. So what happens? On the screen of awareness a few thoughts come through, based on habits that were created in the mind before we knew any better:

I am not there.

Why can't I see this?

When am I going to get it?

Why is this movie happening?

Why do others see this and not me?
…and so on.

The old habit is to give these notions reality or importance. A bit of focus goes onto them and we take them to be true. We believe they are saying something meaningful about who we are. But they are all bogus because they are based on a basic misunderstanding. Once this is pointed out, you start to notice what is going on. You see that your presence—as natural and undeniable awareness—is not touched or threatened in the least. Without effort, the focus or belief falls away through the gentle looking. You easily return to the direct cognition, sense or feeling of pure presence or being. You have never been separate from that. That is a complete impossibility.

Putting the focus on imaginary thoughts just gives the impression that clarity is lost, but it really is not. Even the thoughts are arising right in the clear presence of what you are. Then you may ask, 'But why do these thoughts come up? When will they stop? When will they end?' This is just another string of thoughts, trying to tempt you with the idea that you have a problem and are not 'there'. Do not fall for them and give them any significance.

Thoughts are just ripples in awareness. They are waves in ever-present clarity. Even the thought that thoughts happen is just another thought! From the point of view of presence, it is all just presence. Nothing is really happening. So just question thoughts to see if what they are based on is true. Did you ever separate from the fact of presence-awareness? If not, did you ever really have a problem?

Q: Thank you for your continued feedback and encouragement to me. All is so utterly perfect already. I figure that sooner or later the mind will just get bored with itself.

John: Do not measure yourself by the mind and what is appearing in thought. Thoughts just come and go. You are not creating them or generating them, so why worry about them? They are all based on a simple misperception of what you are, so they are not really valid anyway. Does the sun need to make the clouds change or go away in order to shine? You do not need to do a damn thing with the mind. And there is no need to wait for some endpoint. That is just another subtle concept. Just gently see it. In the seeing, it is dismantled and will not trouble you any longer. The greatest freedom is realizing that you do not need to do anything with the mind. You see that no matter what comes up, it cannot touch who you are. Emphasize what you are more and more. Do not look back at the mind and its states as an indicator of where you are. That is looking in the wrong direction.

You are freedom itself here and now. The mind is only insubstantial images passing on the screen of presence-awareness. Why worry about some shadows? Can they even be there without your light? And if you try to grasp hold of them, do you come up with anything substantial or with any independent existence? Thoughts, being fleeting ripples in awareness, are only awareness themselves. It is like trying to grasp a wave—all you come up with is a fistful of water. So what we are dealing with at all times, whether it be thoughts, feelings or perceptions, is just one substance or reality. That is presence-awareness (or whatever term you prefer), and that is what you are.

93

'I' Is Just a Word

Question: Yesterday evening I was sitting in the kitchen when I sensed a space that needed no explanation and no one to be present. It was presence. It was not a 'mind blower', just a sense and a seeing of sorts. Then I read this piece of yours:

> *'The key is to see that what you are essentially is this field of awareness itself. Awareness is another name for you. That awareness is ever-present and bright, and yet it is no thing that the mind or senses can perceive. It appears to be a space-like emptiness; yet it is brightly aware. This is your nature. Everything else appears in and on this that you are'.*

What jumped out at me was the phrase 'awareness itself'. Though I know that awareness is not an 'it' (an object), we do sense presence. Or do we? 'It is no thing that the mind or senses can perceive' and 'it appears to be a space-like emptiness'. So subtle! As Bob Adamson points out, we rush right by it and carry on with the search.

I am not trying to intellectualize this too much, but I can sense the subtlety of it. I want to be sure not to wallow in a trap. When I sense a thought come up, I ask myself, 'Does awareness change in any way as a result of this thought? Does awareness need any explaining or contextualization? Does anything about it change?' No! The space is, all else changes. I know that all there is is that intelligence-space. But my 'I' is still present in that knowing. The dropping off of questions and ideas happens every time I hear you or Bob Adamson's voice ask, 'Are you aware right now? Seeing? Hearing?'

The mind will whip me silly if I try to work my way through this one. Can you offer any thoughts or suggestions?

John: It is nice to hear from you. You said: 'I know that all there is is that intelligence-space. But my 'I' is still present in that knowing'. What kind of 'I' is there actually? Do not make this overly tricky or subtle. If you do you will be generating a problem where there isn't one. Is there any problem recognizing awareness or your own existence, the simple fact of being? That is what you are. Call it your natural, actual or true self. 'I' is just a word, an idea. You are aware of that idea. It appears right in the space of awareness. It is simple.

The concept 'I', as I use it, is the notion that you exist as some independent, substantial 'thing'—a person, an entity, a someone—apart from pure presence-awareness. To that imaginary entity, the mind adds all kinds of attributes and characteristics. But where is the actual separate entity that is supposedly you? Have you found it yet? Is awareness a body, a mind, an idea, a person? Where is this person that all of our suffering, identifications and doubts are hanging on?

Do not be so quick to say that the 'I' is still present. Did you find anything other than thoughts, feelings and perceptions? And are any of those 'I'? In other words, is there any particular thing that you perceive that you are prepared to grasp hold of and say 'This is what I am'?

You are not the thought 'I'. You are aware of that thought. So what is this aware presence that you are? Can the mind ever know this knower of the mind? And yet do you have any difficulty in recognizing that this is precisely what you are?

Remember, the answer is not in the mind. What is being pointed to can never be grasped or understood at the level of thought. It is too simple! What is being pointed to is just what you are and always have been. The best way to take this is just to stop and notice what is being pointed to. Then simply abide in and as this ever-present true nature. If you begin to conceptualize about it, it appears to elude you. Still, you can never lose your true nature. It is the simple fact of being and awareness that is constantly with you.

94

Quiet Joy and Sparkling Peacefulness

Question: I just read your recent note to the person who is worried that he is getting old and will never get 'it'. Your answer here (and elsewhere)—to just return to fundamentals—is right on. It reminds me of Bankei, the old Zen teacher. All he ever talked about was the Unborn (as he called it).

I wanted to offer a personal note. I am an old guy too, 50 years old. I had been chasing this since I was 18. The final acceptance came through your simple pointing at what is. I threw away my books, my practices, my doubts and my worries. And I laugh a lot more! I think it is especially hard, as Ramana pointed out, for intellectuals to get how dumb simple this is. I was an especially tough nut to crack, just because I love to think, and thinking is not our natural state. But not taking thoughts seriously leaves a big gap, and I think that is the fear for many. They think, 'What will I do with myself if I do not have to chase thoughts anymore?' For me, I have found a lot of pleasure in a life without books and seeking. Like the character in 'Groundhog Day', I seem to have an infinite amount of free time. I am learning to play kirtans on the guitar, singing thanks and praise to the bright awareness that illuminates all. What remains is quiet joy and a sparkling peacefulness—a sweet way to grow old! Thanks and love.

John: Thank you for the beautiful note. I always enjoy hearing about how people are able to take these pointers to heart and gain the understanding for themselves. That is what this is all about. There is nothing to give and nothing to get. There is only a coming back to what is clear, simple and obvious right in you. We just overlooked it. But when pointed out directly and without frills, you recognize what you never lost. 'Sailor' Bob Adamson helped me to see this for myself. It is hard not to keep from sharing the good news. You, in turn, will naturally touch others who may be interested in this message.

95

Accept Your Inherent, Already Perfect Goodness

Question: I have read in your articles and also heard someone at your last meeting talk about things 'falling away'. I have heard this term used before. You clearly pointed out that I have realized what is being pointed to, yet nothing of any consequence has really happened. I feel as though the search need not go on, but I have the expectation that a lot of beliefs are going to be seen through. I do not want to replace my old false expectations with new ones. Can you offer any guidance?

John: What I am pointing to is that your identity is the simple fact of being-awareness. Contrary to popular belief this is clearly known and recognized right now. There is nothing difficult about seeing or knowing what you are. Everything else that comes up in the nature of a doubt, question, problem or feeling of personal suffering would only be due to an unexamined belief, a notion that you are something apart from what you truly are. This needs to be thoroughly seen and understood. It is not difficult, but it needs to be done. Beliefs fall away through scrutiny and questioning.

You speak of expectations. See this as a subtle concept. It implies waiting or looking for something you do not have. Do you need this idea? Why expect anything at all when everything you can possibly seek is already present as what you are?

Certainly, I encourage you not to replace old beliefs with new ones. It is good that you see this! When you do not grasp onto or give credence to any idea whatsoever and simply rest in and as pure presence-awareness, is there anything wrong with that state, that recognition? Get to know that clear, bright and ever-present sense of being-awareness. It appears subtle to the mind, but it contains such a joy and sweetness that as you get a feel for it you will realize that there is no need to go to the mind to seek anything at all. Accept your inherent, already perfect goodness. There has never been a problem with that. It is free, complete, and whole right from the start.

Q: Thank you. I do not think the notion of separation has been clearly seen through.

John: Well, just see that as another belief. Why grab hold of even that? I assure you that you are fine just as you are! The expressway to your ever-present state of inherent perfection is to relinquish all contrary ideas, especially the one that says you are not yet there.

96

You Were Always in Search of Yourself

Question: It is curious this spontaneous attraction to you. Sometimes it feels like you are myself in a very palpable way—just that awareness. At other times, there is an identification with the forms and the concepts. The resonance is the bridge. I wanted to go to India and Europe in search for one who would awaken that resonance and who could help with this 'seeing clearly'. It may change, I do not know, but the search was over when I read the first few lines in your book, and you persist in my mind's eye and heart as a doorway into the true Self.

John: There is just a pointing to what you were already searching for and intuitively knew to be true. You were always in search of yourself. Now this is clear. This resonance in the recognition of what is true can be helpful. It certainly was helpful for me. It gave me the faith or confidence to look and see for myself what was being pointed to. The important thing is your direct understanding of what is being pointed to. This is the essence and focus.

Q: Some things are verified facts—that I am awareness, that the separate person does not exist in reality, that there is identification with a number of imaginings still present and calling themselves 'I', and that there is a 'character' that believes it can, with a little help, sort this whole thing out.

John: This is just the residual belief that such a character exists. Surprisingly, when you actually look for it, you cannot find anything like that at all. It is the belief in the existence of that character that drives the imaginings and identification.

My advice is not to worry about the imaginings and the identifications of the character. Rather, put the focus on examining that root assumption. Is there a separate self in the picture at all? If that is dealt with, all of the other issues are resolved automatically and effortlessly.

Q: During the day, when remembrance occurs, all that I do is discard, one after the other, the known thoughts that, by habit, assert my identity as a separate entity.

John: This is good. Just see these thoughts for what they are—simply thoughts. They are residual habits based on beliefs that we picked up along the way, not knowing any better. That is all that is going on. Then come back to the simple noticing that what you are is not a thought at all. It is the simple, undeniable presence of awareness that you have now seen. This combination of seeing the falseness of the ideas and the presence of what is clear and true in you will dismantle the beliefs and diffuse the energy going into the thoughts. They drop away spontaneously because the unexamined notions fueling them have been exposed. Your ever-present nature of pure clarity stands out all the more clearly. In truth, it is always there and is not ever touched by the appearances. Seeing this, the game is up. The rise and fall of thoughts is of no consequence whatsoever.

Q: Many times things get muddy because there is some heavy and sticky emotion, or some very subtle but binding emotion. There does not seem to be any discernible thought pattern, which makes it difficult to be the shining awareness behind them or even to see clearly that the separate person is the culprit. And when all this mind play is seen, there is only a desire to be very, very quiet because it all feels like lifting oneself by one's shoestrings. Sometimes there is a relaxing and the feeling that there is nothing wrong becomes a reality.

John: Just notice that no matter how sticky or heavy the thoughts or emotions, they are all just appearances arising in the space of bright awareness that you are. Do not fall into the trap that you need to make those things go away. Put the emphasis on what is clear and present. Emphasize your true nature rather than looking to the appearances as a sign for where you stand. Recognition of your ever-free state is natural and simple. The feeling is more of a non-doing, a simple understanding, a relaxation into what is already present and clear. With this, the energy ceases to flow into thoughts and they come to balance of themselves. From there you can also have a good look at the thoughts to see if their basis is true. You do not have to get rid of shadows to see the light of the sun. You just turn in the direction of the sun and see its light. The light of reality is your own presence, your own being. That is what is always present, knowing all the thoughts and feelings.

Thoughts Cannot Know Awareness

Question: I just do not seem to be getting it. I think I might be using my mind too much. But how do I look at awareness without using my mind?

John: What you are sensing is true. The mind is not a factor in recognizing awareness. It is completely the wrong tool. That is all. We are used to using the mind to understand. It works well for many things. But it is not very useful in the direct recognition of your true nature of awareness. Awareness knows thoughts, but thoughts cannot know awareness. If we turn to the mind to recognize who we are, we overlook the simplicity of it. Your true being of existence-awareness is clearly known and present right now, without effort.

There is no need to look for awareness. It is simply pointed out that awareness is already present and that is what you are. It is a simple statement of fact. It is not a prescription to then go out and search for it. That view generates an unnecessary problem. The question 'How do I look at awareness?' is very interesting. It presumes you are one thing and awareness is something else. It also presumes that there is a need for a technique or method to see it. But that is a misunderstanding. Just see that as a mistaken concept.

When I ask you if you are aware, the answer is spontaneous and effortless. You already know it! Once you know what you are, you can look at any residual concepts or false beliefs, see them for what they are and discard them. You simply notice that the ideas are asserting something about you that is not true. Just seeing the ideas as false is enough. They drop away spontaneously because you no longer believe in them.

Belief Systems Lead to Suffering

Question: This morning, upon learning of the recent terrorist attacks in London, I am once again reminded of the appearance of evil and evil people within our world.

John: The notions of 'evil' and 'evil people' are extremely slippery concepts. As I see it, all beings are motivated by their conditioned belief systems. Standards of morality are local and conditional. One side suffers and one side rejoices based on the respective belief systems. All belief systems ultimately lead to suffering at some level.

Q: Having lived through the horror of September 11, I now feel thrown back into a muddle of egoic reactions, from heart-break to fear to intense anger and outrage. And all this from a 'personality' which prides itself on being 'anti-war' and peace loving.

John: These are noble stances, no doubt, but they are still belief systems. In the grand scheme of things there is no particular advantage in being for or against war or any other concept. You must still return to fundamentals—knowing who you are. Beliefs for or against something do not get you any nearer to the immediate recognition of who you are.

Q: In the years following September 11, our leaders have used the rhetoric of ridding the world of 'evil doers'. The evil doers in this case are of a religious sort who appear to act from a distorted spiritual perspective of God and free-will. Since that September morning I have come to a new insight and understanding of non-duality. I thought I had an understanding of the nature of non-doership. But now I feel lost and confused. Perhaps I am writing this in the heat of the moment, having apparently fallen back into the hypnotic trance of separation.

John: Just ask yourself if throughout any of this the basic fact of your identity as that which is present and aware has gone anywhere. A few old beliefs or patterns of thought may have surfaced due to circumstances, but nothing has touched the innate fact of being.

Q: I do see that these emotions and perceptions are arising within awareness. I see that the sense of being a separate self asking this question also arises within awareness. But this insight does not bring peace this morning. The issues of 'free-will' and 'evil' still seem to be a wrench in the mind's ability to understand the question 'why?' Of course, this is why the answers to this and all questions cannot be resolved at the level of thought.

John: Free-will and evil are purely imaginary concepts. They are created by the mind and overlaid on immediate, non-conceptual experience, which is utterly free of them.

Awareness is peace itself. Peace is not to be brought in. The mind will never understand 'why?' because it is a false question. The mind imagines time, space, causality, right, wrong, individuals, free-will and so on. Not a single one of these things is given in immediate experience. Having created the notion of causality (or the notion that there is a 'why') we go in search for an answer to 'why?' There is no 'why' because time, causality, and agency are illusions. They are just concepts. So, 'why' is an imaginary problem. There is no adequate solution to an imaginary problem. The best course is to expose the problem as false, rather than look for an answer that cannot be found.

Q: The people who commit these acts of terrorism have no choice in what they do? The people who are victims of these acts of terrorism had no choice but to be a victim of those acts? It is all God's will? There are no terrorists or victims? There is only one Self which appears to be playing the roles of terrorists and victims and this person who questions it all? Nothing is really happening? It is only a dream (nightmare) within awareness which remains untouched by the current events which appear to be happening within it?

John: People, victims, terrorists, god, god's will, persons, nightmares—these are all concepts created in thought. They are makeshift words designed for purposes of communication. Our only fault is that we take them to be realities. All the focus on these concepts takes the attention away from the ever-present light of pure awareness or presence or love. From the perspective of who you truly are, the world as a separate entity unto itself has really never existed. Even if the appearance is granted, it does not contradict the presence of your real being. So nothing is lost. You never move away from pure love and clear presence—even in the midst of the greatest apparent tragedy.

You ask why there is suffering. The answer is clear. Imagining oneself as a separate being or person leads to isolation and fear. Then the mind grasps hold of some convenient definitions and beliefs as a way out of the imagined bondage. This leads to all manner of confused ideas and actions—some classified as horrible. The ultimate cause is ignorance. Beings who commit crimes and harm others are miserable themselves, due to a lack of self-knowledge. They perpetuate these actions out of misguided attempts to secure happiness.

You Have Never Been a Separate Self

Question: This morning the understanding of presence of awareness hit me. It was not a thunderbolt. It was just an 'OK, then!' All day I have been sensing it and savoring it—neither disbelieving nor believing that this is it. It just is. Then I notice it in various ways, more from what it is not and what does not come up. I even toss up some old sacred concepts like mental tennis balls just to see if the mind will have a whack and start the game again. So far only whiffs.

This is odd. It is simple. I will write more soon as I see and savor this, and as I believe it really and truly. All is in this presence, awareness.

John: Stay in touch about how things are settling in. What you are saying sounds good. Awareness or presence is just who you are. That is it. You have never been an individual separate self. That assumption was the root of the problem. Once that is pointed out you can come to this understanding directly for yourself. This is what you are doing. Keep things simple and direct.

All doubts, questions and problems are traceable to the notion that you have separated from your real being. If any of those things come up, investigate the root cause and see if it is true. Where is the separate self at the root of all problems? Did you ever find one? So it is all an optical illusion. The whole structure falls to pieces upon investigation. You discover that you are and always have been that light of presence-awareness, which is the source of freedom, joy, peace and reality. See this thoroughly and all seeking and searching is done.

Conceptual Knowledge Does Not Yield Joy

Question: Things are still unfolding quite nicely. I absolutely see what I am and what I am not. It is very clear. It does seem to be coming in bits and pieces.

John: This is fine. Various facets fall into place and are understood. However, you can also see that what is being pointed to—the fact of your own being—is already present and fully clear. It does not come in at once or in bits in pieces, because it is already present.

Q: I just drove back from a trip. It was dark and I did not realize there was a train coming along side the road. All of a sudden, it blew its horns. The physical body jumped a foot and there was a brief moment of looking for an oncoming train. I heard the words, 'God, that really scared me'. But the actual experience was of this powerful electric energy that shot through the body. It had no label of fear. There was sensation before I labeled it, just an intense physical sensation. Then I (awareness) saw the conceptual 'I' arise and label it as fear. And it was so clear that the whole experience was just an appearance in the awareness, and not something happening to a 'someone'.

John: Excellent. The concept of the existence of a 'someone' is seen as false. This undercuts the whole network of suffering. How can self-centered thoughts survive, if there is no separate self? They only survived as long as this idea was taken as true.

Q: I could see that what I am preceded both the experience and the self-centered 'I' that was fearful. These more direct experiences of seeing are happening more and more.

John: Excellent.

Q: I often stop to notice that I am pure awareness and see that there is always some sensation and thought appearing in awareness. For a while there was just this ordinary experience of noticing that I was present and aware. Now this noticing is sometimes accompanied by arising joy and peace.

John: This is good. Mere conceptual knowledge does not yield joy or peace. As you continue to recognize your identity as presence-awareness, the natural joy and peace inherent in that comes to the forefront. It has always been there, but it was just overlooked because the focus was on the mental static, instead of just relaxing with the natural state of presence-awareness, which is what you are.

Q: I can see quite clearly that the 'I' is just an idea or thought which arises. It has its moment and then disappears. There is nothing more than that. Likewise, the body becomes less and less subjective and more and more an apparatus in my peripheral vision. It seems to be doing its own thing without my interference or direction. It is very strange at times. I had no idea the body did so many things without my noticing!

There certainly are periods when there is much thought that is jumping right into all sorts of relational experiences. And there is still some physical or emotional reaction to the thought. But soon it is seen that those are just strings of thought with no reality of their own, even though there may be some residual bodily emotion or feeling associated with them. And the more self-centered the thought, the more likely there is to be an emotion.

That is my update for now. I am quite content at this point just to watch it all happen. I may be fully baked, but I seem to want the experience of watching the whole baking process unfold!

John: All this is good. If there is any unfolding it is happening in the ever-free and clear presence that you are. Awareness and the recognition of your nature as that is not a process. It is the necessary background of any process or unfolding. How many processes or unfoldings could you have if you were not present and aware to register them? That presence-awareness is fully here now. It is what you are and always have been. See it now or later, all at once or in bits and pieces, or do not see it at all—still you cannot deny the fact of what you are. Nothing is achieved—only the simple recognition of who you have been all along.

101

Is There Any Moment One Is Not Oneself?

Question: Whenever one is not being oneself …

John: Is there any moment one is not oneself?

Q: I realize it is impossible to stop being what one already is. Nevertheless, one seems to lose recognition of oneself when there is identification with the story 'I am a body born in time'.

John: Still, does an imaginary story really change who you are? Once you see that it is an imaginary story, you are done with it. It is the belief that it is real that keeps us focused on it.

Q: This story continues to repeat itself. But at any point within it, we can recall our no-thingness.

John: True, but why not just see that the story is false? Then there is no need to remember anything. Our being cannot be recalled. A recollection is a memory, which is just a thought. We are whether we attempt to remember it or not.

Q: So from the original perspective we are just being ourselves effortlessly and enjoying our own timeless being as the space in which everything happens.

John: Always! Eventually, you just see the simple truth of it.

Q: I think this seeing has happened with me recently but I tend to wander off downstream all the time, even as I write this.

John: Seemingly, but did you actually leave your own being, your own awareness? Even when apparently caught or lost, you have not lost who you are. See this thoroughly and there is no more getting or losing anything.

Q: Up until now, my search has been a process of coming across an essential concept, such as 'there is no one inside' or 'I am being lived by life' and using this concept to live from, to re-orient my perception back to what I believe it should be. The problem, though, has been that inevitably the concept loses its efficacy and 'zap'. Or I simply forget it. Then I am lost until I find another one. But each time, I feel that I am getting closer. I have felt that I have needed to find a concept that is so all-embracing and perfect that it will remain valid and effective as a pointer forever. But this has not happened yet. Now I am noticing that this will never work.

John: Excellent. Mental insights and slogans eventually run dry. What you are is not a thought or concept. True self-knowledge is not a mental experience or a result of holding onto a concept, however noble. It is the immediate, non-conceptual recognition of your nature as presence-awareness.

Q: A few days ago when I was reading one of your articles, I suddenly saw the obvious fact that I am the presence in which everything happens. I am the fundamental. I have always suspected this and felt this but now it is seen as absolutely real and makes sense of everything. In a sense, I have finally married my deepest intuition with the outside world—in this case, the words of another human being.

John: A pointer to the simple and obvious fact of what you are struck home. The pointer is the least important. You have followed it and seen the facts for yourself. That is all that matters.

Q: Now, I am just trying to catch myself, to notice my misidentification, and thus return to presence as often as I can.

John: Do this a few times and then you will recognize the fact that you never leave presence. Never having left it, there is no need to return to it. Then you just settle in with the recognition of what you are and have always been.

Q: I am trying to tamper less with things and problems, with decisions and uncertainties. I try to move away from thoughts and their hypnotic effects and to return to my ever-present freedom. Does this sound right to you? It is a great help to have your guidance.

John: Yes. Give up the focus on thoughts, problems and other mind stuff that hinges on the belief that you are some limited being apart from the deeper truth. You are not, and so those thoughts are groundless. You will not gain much from attending to baseless and false thoughts! Return to your ever-present freedom, if you need to, until you see that it is indeed ever-present. Then you see why it is called the natural state.

102

Presence-Awareness Is Already Known

Question: I was in London two weeks back and just stumbled across your book 'The Natural State' at Watkins Bookstore. I started reading it last week. This is different and literally mind blowing. The way you have worded the message is so powerful and direct. Nothing like this happened to me previously! I could actually see glimpses of the presence-awareness that you are referring to. But this was only while reading. Now I am back again in my old experience. You will say 'Who is saying this?' I understand that this insight into presence-awareness is a sudden event and, more importantly, a permanent event.

John: This is reasonable but not precisely true. Presence-awareness is an already present fact. It is already known (who does not know they are present and aware?). Yet the significance of it is not understood. We were living in a false dream of being someone we were not. Then the true position is pointed out. It is just a simple recognition. It is not really an event, but a noticing of something so simple and basic that we overlooked it. It is not as if who you are is not present and then later becomes known. It is just the fact of who you are. So dispense with concepts like sudden or gradual, impermanent or permanent. These will draw you away from the simplicity of what is being pointed out. It is much simpler than we imagine.

Q: It seems that once you see this, there is no looking back after that. If so, then what is the significance of the temporary and transient occurrences that happened to me while reading your book? Are they illusions, or are they the play of the mind?

John: You are recognizing what is being pointed to. There is a recognition of the truth of who you are. Through force of habit, the mind comes in again and the focus goes back into the false beliefs of who we are. But once this message strikes home, there is a natural drawing to abide in and as your true state. The recognition of who you are comes to the fore and the focus on the false concepts falls out of the picture. The net result is that the simple recognition your true nature dawns. It is not an attainment because it was never missing. It was just overlooked. The recognition of it is natural, simple and direct.

103

The Absence That Is Full

Question: I have only just discovered your book, and what a pleasure it has been to read! For me, it did not so much inform as confirm. Some time ago I had a sudden insight that I had never really lived a life at all. I had simply been living my thoughts—one thought reacting to another—and making of the result something it decided to call a 'life'. It knocked me back a bit, and I am glad to say I have never fully recovered! I realized that I had always been the one indescribable thing that was looking out my eyes in precisely the same way in middle-age as it had been in childhood. There was not one iota of difference. An alleged 'life' had been lived around what I was, but had never represented my actual nature. It had only seemed influential through a bogus recognition. With the recognition gone, there was no life to live—nor had there ever been. The imagined world was built on no more than misguided distinctions.

I cannot say this has left me in any particular mystical state. On the contrary, it seems incredibly ordinary. As I think the 'Tao Te Ching' comments at some point when describing the Tao: 'It is blank, uninteresting, without color—yet you cannot get enough of it'.

Your book implied that everything had already happened—or perhaps rather that there was never a need for anything to happen. I liked that very much. Thought, given a chance, will of course split life into little parcels of experience, cajoling us into approaching them separately, but if everything is present, the obvious corollary is that nothing is. That absence is so full there is simply no room for anything else, and that one acknowledgement puts the whole world to rest.

Once again, my real thanks for the book.

John: Nice to hear from you. You have said it all beautifully. It looks like the fundamental understanding is clear for you. I am glad the book has been helpful as a confirmation of your innate knowing. Feel free to stay in touch if you like.

ABOUT THE PUBLISHER

Non-Duality Press publishes book and audio resources on the theme of non-duality and *Advaita* with particular emphasis on works by contemporary speakers and authors.

For an up-to-date catalogue of books and CDs, with online ordering please visit: www. non-dualitybooks.com.

Other titles from Non-Duality Press include:

Awakening to the Natural State &
Right Here, Right Now: John Wheeler

What's Wrong with Right Now? &
Presence-Awareness: 'Sailor' Bob Adamson

From Self to Self &
Awakening to the Dream: Leo Hartong

Already Awake &
Being: the bottom line: Nathan Gill

I Am Life Itself: Unmani Liza Hyde

I Hope You Die Soon: Richard Sylvester